RELIGIOUS LIFE
and
COMMUNITIES

KETER BOOKS

This book is compiled from material originally published
in the *Encyclopaedia Judaica*

Copyright © 1974, Keter Publishing House Jerusalem Ltd.
P.O.Box 7145, Jerusalem, Israel

Cat. No. 25071

ISBN 0 7065 1329 0

Printed in Israel

CONTENTS

CONTRIBUTORS

Misha Louvish; Writer and Journalist, Jerusalem

Mordechai Hacohen (*deceased*); Jerusalem

Benjamin Zvieli; Rabbi, Director of Religious Broadcasting, Jerusalem

Schalom Ben-Chorin; Writer and Journalist, Jerusalem

Jacob Yehoshua; Former Director of the Muslim Department, Ministry of Religious Affairs, Jerusalem

Prof. Chaim Wardi; Professor of Christianity in the Middle East and Africa, Tel Aviv University

Prof. Haim Blanc; Professor of Linguistics, the Hebrew University of Jerusalem

Judge Henry Eli Baker; President of the District Court, Jerusalem; Research Fellow in the Law Faculty, the Hebrew University of Jerusalem

Prof. Menachem Elon; Advocate, Rabbi, Professor of Jewish Law and Director of the Institute for Research in Jewish Law, the Hebrew University of Jerusalem

Dr. Aharon Layish; Lecturer in the Department of History of Muslim Countries, Institute of Asian and African Studies, the Hebrew University of Jerusalem

Dr. Louis Isaac Rabinowitz; Rabbi, Deputy Editor in Chief of *Encyclopaedia Judaica*, former Chief Rabbi of the Transvaal and former Professor of Hebrew, the University of the Witwatersrand, Johannesburg. Jerusalem

Dr. Raphael Posner; Rabbi, Deputy Editor in Chief of *Encyclopaedia Judaica*, Assistant Professor of Rabbinics, the Jewish Theological Seminary of America, Jerusalem

Dr. James W. Parkes; Historian, Blandford, Dorset, England

Dr. Saul Paul Colbi; Advisor on Christian Affairs to the Minister of Religious Affairs, Jerusalem

Jacob Auerbach; Jerusalem

Prof. Shmuel Safrai; Professor of Jewish History, the Hebrew University of Jerusalem

Semah Cecil Hyman; Former Minister Plenipotentiary, Ministry for Foreign Affairs, Jerusalem

INTRODUCTION

The entry of the Land of Israel into modern history in the 19th century was closely connected with its religious significance as the cradle of Judaism and Christianity. While the great powers were motivated mainly by strategic and economic considerations in their efforts to establish and increase their influence in the country, it was the presence of various religious communities, especially the Christian denominations, that provided them with the occasion and the means to gain a foothold. Russia, for example, had long had rights over Greek-Orthodox holy places in Palestine and France had rights to protect the Latin (Catholic) Church. Britain and Prussia tried to counter these advantages by extending their protection to the tiny Protestant minority, and the former, from Palmerston onward, sought to extend unofficial protection to the Jews.

Under Ottoman rule, there was a close correlation between religious and national identity. The *millets,* or religious communities, were corporate entities with quasi-national characteristics, enjoying a measure of internal autonomy—particularly in matters of personal status, like marriage, divorce, and inheritance, which were under the jurisdiction of their respective Religious Courts.

These concepts and their legal consequences were partially carried over into the period of the British Mandate and, to some extent, they still affect life and law in the State of Israel. "Jew" is legally recognized as both a religious and a national designation; practically all Muslims (as well as most Christians) are Arabs; the Druze community is also both religious and national in character. Israel law still recognizes the jurisdiction of the various Religious Courts in certain matters of personal status.

It should be noted, however, that these powers depend for their continued validity on legislation enacted by the Knesset, the democratically elected parliament, which could withdraw all or any of them by a majority decision. If a question of conflicting jurisdictions arises, moreover, the Supreme Court may rule on the competence of the Religious Courts to deal with a particular matter.

Ever since the reestablishment of Jewish independence, much thought has been devoted to the problems arising out of the unique position of Israel as the secular state of a people whose national survival has always been closely bound up with its religious traditions. Questions of Sabbath observance, religious education and marriage and divorce law have frequently given rise to heated controversy between the religiously observant minority and the non-observant majority. Religious issues have an important influence on political affairs: religious parties represent some 15% of the electorate and may hold the balance in government coalitions. Israel's religious life also plays a significant role in its relations with Diaspora Jewry. In recent years the fundamental question of Jewish identity—whether Jewish national affiliation can be decided by non-religious criteria—has come to the fore.

At the end of 1972, out of a total population of 3,200,500 in Israel (including the whole of Jerusalem but not the Israel-administered areas), there were 2,723,600 Jews, 358,600 Muslims, 79,600 Christians, and 38,700 Druze and others. In addition, there were about 610,000 Muslims in Judea and Samaria and 390,000 in the Gaza Strip and Northern Sinai, 30,000 Christians in Judea and Samaria (mostly in Bethlehem) and some 6,000 Druze in the Golan Heights.

Israel's population reflects, therefore, a veritable mosaic, composed of the Jewish majority and a wide range of religious-ethnic minority communities. This book is an attempt to present in a concise form this colorful and unique phenomenon in its various aspects.

Part One:

RELIGIOUS LIFE
AND COMMUNITIES

1 JEWS

At the end of 1972, there were 2,723,600 Jews in Israel, 85% of the population (including the whole of Jerusalem but not the Israel-administered areas).

UNDER THE OTTOMAN RULE. The Jews of the pre-Zionist old *yishuv*, both Sephardim (from the Orient) and Ashkenazim (of European origin), dedicated their lives to the fulfillment of religious precepts: the study of the Torah and the meticulous observance of its commandments; prayer at the holy sites for the coming of the Messiah and interment of their remains in the Holy Land to await his advent. They lived apart—mainly in the holy cities of Jerusalem, Hebron, Safed, and Tiberias—under the authority of their rabbis and religious courts (*battei din*) which dealt essentially with civil disputes as well as problems of *halakhah,* with their own autonomous educational, charitable, and social institutions. Many of the most renowned Jewish religious scholars of the time were to be found in the old *yishuv.* Indeed, religious learning was so widespread that even the humblest possessed a basic knowledge of the Torah, if not more.

Communal Organization. While the *yishuv* was still very small, Ashkenazim and Sephardim prayed together and occasionally intermarried. As the number of Ashkenazi immigrants increased, however, the two communities moved apart, while the Ashkenazim were divided among themselves according to their respective lands of origin. Social and political conditions under Ottoman rule militated against the participation of the Jewish population in the 3 economic life of the country. Moreover, many of the immigrants were elderly people who had come to the Holy Land to be buried there, and there was a high proportion of widows and orphans. Hence, the old *yishuv* had to depend for its sustenance upon contributions from abroad, known as *ḥalukkah*.

Accordingly, in every community there were subcommunities called *kolelim* (or *kolelot*), each with its *va'ad*, (committee), which distributed the funds received from its place of origin. This was the only form of communal

Seal of the Hebron Sephardi community, 1865, with the cave of Machpelah in the center. From O. Avisar (ed.), *Sefer Ḥevron*, Jerusalem, 1970.

organization that existed at the time. At the turn of the century, there were Sephardi *kolelim* of Jews from North Africa, Georgia, Persia, Aleppo, Iraq, Bukhara, Daghestan, Afghanistan, and Yemen. The Ashkenazim were even more fragmented. They were not only divided into Ḥasidim and *Perushim* (descendants of disciples of Elijah of Vilna[1]), but subdivided into over 30 *kolelim*, which maintained the only registers of births and deaths, marriages and divorces. Each *kolel* kept to itself; each prospered or declined in proportion to the support it received from its parent community in the Diaspora. Although the total amount contributed may have been increased by the splintering, the resultant dissension impeded the development of the *yishuv*.

Aware of the neglect of the common good caused by the proliferation of the *kolelim* and influenced by the dominant personality of Rabbi Samuel Salant,[2] the rabbis and communal leaders of the Jerusalem Ashkenazi community established in 1866 an overall committee of all *kolelim*, which they named Keneset Yisrael. Its functions were: to handle the affairs of the Ashkenazim in Jerusalem, especially the payment of taxes to the government; to distribute *ḥalukkah* funds to families not belonging to any of the *kolelim*; and to provide help in special individual cases. Its income was derived from funds collected in countries not connected with any specific *kolel*, such as the United States, Great Britain, and South Africa.

The supervision of *sheḥitah* (ritual slaughter) to ensure perfect *kashrut* was a matter of great concern, as in any Orthodox Jewish community. At first, complete control was in the hands of the Sephardim, but in 1864 the *hakham bashi* (chief rabbi) was persuaded to allow the creation of a separate *sheḥitah* board for the Ashkenazi community in Jerusalem. The fees paid for its certification became an important source of revenue for the Ashkenazi rabbis and

---

[1] The Vilna Gaon, outstanding spiritual and intellectual leader of Jewry (1720-1797)

[2] Chief rabbi of Jerusalem (1816-1905)

other religious functionaries. In the other cities Sephardim and Ashkenazim also kept their *sheḥitah* separate.

Like the *kolelim,* the voluntary burial societies became more and more fragmented as time went on. At first all interments took place in the ground owned by the Sephardim on the Mount of Olives, but in 1858 the Ashkenazim acquired their own section on the mount and established a separate burial society. Important as a source of revenue from legacies and the sale of plots, the burial societies became the adjuncts of the various *kolelim,* and to this day there is a multiplicity of such societies in Jerusalem.

The Rabbinate and its Courts. Supreme religious and judicial authority was vested in the *ḥakham bashi* of Jerusalem, also entitled *rishon le-Zion,* who was elected by the leaders of the local Sephardi community. On the recommendation of the *ḥakham bashi* of the Ottoman Empire, he received a firman from the Sublime Porte appointing him official representative of the Jewish community of the Holy Land in its dealings with the government and investing him with authority over all Jewish spiritual and religious affairs. He and his courts had exclusive jurisdiction in matters of matrimony, personal status, charitable trusts, certification of wills, and legacies of all Jewish Ottoman subjects. His investiture was marked by a solemn ceremony conducted in the R. Johanan b. Zakkai Synagogue in Jerusalem. In the discharge of his functions, he was assisted by two committees: one consisting of Sephardi rabbinical judges, for religious affairs; the other, composed of lay communal leaders, for dealing with the government, etc.

The office was held by Raphael Meir Panigel (1879–93) and then by Jacob Saul b. Eliezer Elyashar (1893–1906). R. Elyashar's death was followed by a virulent controversy over the succession. When R. Ya'akov Meir, who, in addition to his rabbinic knowledge, had studied languages and sciences on his own, was elected by a majority, the conservative section of the community vigorously opposed him and he consequently left the country and accepted the post of chief rabbi in Smyrna. In 1907 the more progressive element elected R. Eliyahu-Moshe Panigel, who had studied for a while at the modern Laemmel school, but he was forced to resign in 1908 and was replaced by R. Naḥman Batito, who held the office until his death in 1915. In the following year R. Nissim Yehudah Danon was elected, but he relinquished his post in 1918, and no further appointment was made until the official establishment of the Chief Rabbinate in 1921.

The Ashkenazim, who for the most part were foreign nationals, conducted their own rabbinic courts and maintained their own educational and philanthropic institutions. In practice, the large *kolelim* were autonomous, and the *ḥakham bashi* made no effort to interfere. R. Samuel Salant was recognized as the undisputed head of the Ashkenazi community in Jerusalem for almost 70 years (1841–1909), as it grew from 500 to 30,000 souls, though he refused to accept any formal appointment. His enormous erudition and piety earned him the deference of the Sephardim as well. He curbed dissension and also the opposition of the old *yishuv* to the new. As he became weakened by advancing age, he appointed R. Eliyahu David Rabinovich Teomim (known as "the *ADeReT*") in 1901 to assist him as head of the *bet din* of the Ashkenazi community of Jerusalem, but the latter died in 1903. On the death of R. Samuel Salant in 1909, R. Ḥayyim Berlin assumed the title and held it until his death in 1915. No new appointment could be made during W.W.1. In 1895 Shneur Zalman Laderer of Lublin, who had settled in Jerusalem, founded, together with local ḥasidic dignitaries, a ḥasidic *bet din* in the city, which functioned in harmony with that of the Ashkenazi majority. In the Sephardi communities, too, separate rabbinic courts emerged for the Moroccan and Yemenite communities. In Safed, Tiberias, and Hebron, the Ashkenazi and Sephardi rabbinates conducted their respective religious courts.

Decisions in all matters, civil and religious, public and private, were rendered in accordance with the law of the Torah. The litigants willingly submitted to the verdicts of the *battei din;* very rarely was it necessary to compel a   7 recalcitrant to comply with a court order by withholding his *ḥalukkah* allotment or imposing some other penalty. Deviations from orthodoxy could be punished by the imposition of the *ḥerem* ("ban"), which was invoked against many prominent rabbis and notable persons. In 1886 R. Naphtali Herz ha-Levi Weidenbaum was sent from Jerusalem to be rabbi of the growing community in Jaffa. In 1890, the Ashkenazim elected a community council, which was joined by the Sephardim and which conducted its deliberations in Hebrew.

In 1904, R. Abraham Isaac ha-Kohen Kook was appointed rabbi of Jaffa and the surrounding Jewish villages. His was the first appointment made independently of Jerusalem, though he still received his modest salary from Keneset Yisrael, supplemented by fees from the Rishon le-Zion wine cellars for his certificate of *kashrut*. His appointment created a veritable revolution in Jewish religious life. He was the first outstanding rabbi in Erez Israel who was a Zionist. His strong character, rabbinic erudition, and mastery of philosophic and mystic teachings enabled him to pursue his own independent course. Holding that even the least religious of the new settlers had been motivated by deep, subconscious religious impulses to become pioneers in the Land of Israel and that secular Zionism would therefore ultimately become religious, he treated the nonobservant with respect and affection, proffering them his warm friendship. To the new *yishuv* he was an inspiration, and even the most doughty anti-Zionists among the old had to treat him with respect. R. Ben-Zion Meir Ḥai Ouziel, appointed Sephardi chief rabbi of Jaffa in 1912, was also an avowed Zionist. Having gone abroad to attend a world conference of Agudat Israel in 1914, Rabbi Kook was prevented from returning to Jaffa by the outbreak of World War I.

Education. The yeshivot were of the same pattern as their Diaspora counterparts, except that in the Holy Land heads of families and even the elderly continued to study and draw students' stipends in addition to their regular *halukkah* allocations. In the earliest-founded villages, the farmers' sons would study Torah in the evenings, generally with the local *shohatim* as teachers. Between 1900 and 1905 a few more progressive *hadarim* were founded, and R. Zerah Braverman, head of the Me'ah She'arim Yeshivah, together with his associates, established *talmud torahs* where secular subjects were taught in conformity with the spirit of Jewish tradition.

Shemittah. A new issue erupted as the result of the existence of Jewish farming villages. The sabbatical year (*shemittah*) 5649 (1888/89), when Jewish law required farmers to leave their fields fallow, was approaching. The question arose as to whether they must actually abstain from cultivating their fields or could evade the prohibition by the legal device of having the land "sold" formally to a non-Jew. The Jerusalem rabbis adamantly opposed the formal sale of the land. Some of the settlers abstained from all work, some relied on the rabbinically prepared bill of sale, others openly defied the *shemittah* laws. The debate was acrimonious and prolonged, growing more intense from one sabbatical year to the next. For the year 5670 (1909/10), Rabbi Kook himself arranged the bill of sale and the conflict reached its peak. The Ashkenazi rabbis of the old *yishuv* endeavored to enlist support all over the world against anything but the complete cessation of all work on the land, although Rabbi Kook pleaded that such rigid adherence to the restrictions would threaten the very existence of the Jewish villages.

UNDER THE BRITISH MANDATE. *The New Yishuv Expands.* From 1919 onward the texture of the *yishuv* began to change, as large numbers of immigrants streamed in; ten or fifteen years later the new *yishuv* had, in numbers, overtaken and surpassed the old. Many of the middle-class families who arrived from Eastern Europe were religious, some Hasidim. They gravitated toward Tel Aviv and Haifa, where they founded their synagogues and other religious institutions in the traditional mode. They differed from the old *yishuv*, however, in their positive attitude to organized 9 communal life and their western clothing. Many of them filled the ranks of the Orthodox Agudat Israel movement and established its educational system. The Yemenite immigrants who flocked to the newer settlements, especially to Jaffa and Tel Aviv, were deeply religious in outlook and feeling. A considerable number of German Jews who arrived during the 1930s were observant Jews, who established synagogues and religious institutions of their own and made their contribution to religious education.

The Chief Rabbinate. With the end of Turkish rule, the office of *hakham bashi* ceased to exist. Furthermore, there had been no president of the Ashkenazi *bet din* of Jerusalem from 1915. On the initiative of Chaim Weizmann and communal leaders the office of the Rabbinate of the Jewish Community in Jerusalem was established with the participation of Sephardi and Ashkenazi rabbis. Its budget was covered by the Zionist Commission with funds provided by the American Jewish Joint Distribution Committee. The British authorities granted some measure of recognition, and the rabbinate functioned both as a court of first instance and as a court of appeal. The Va'ad Kelali (Jerusalem community council) convened a national conference of rabbis and heads of *kolelim,* yeshivot, and other institutions, which invited Rabbi Kook, who was about to return to the country, to become president of the *bet din* and chief rabbi of Jerusalem. His former antagonists bitterly opposed the nomination, but he accepted the position. Rabbi Kook's prestige and influence extended far beyond the area of his jurisdiction.

Some of the rabbis of Jerusalem, led by R. Yizhak Yeruham Diskin and R. Yosef Hayyim Sonnenfeld, regarded the newly inaugurated rabbinate as a Zionist institution and a disaster for religious Jewry. They went so far as to designate the anniversary of its founding a day of fasting and prayer. They therefore organized their own Ashkenazi council, which later became the *Edah ha-Haredit* ("Orthodox Community") of Agudat Israel, with its own *bet din* (today more or less identical with the Neturei

Karta, who do not recognize the State of Israel). In 1920 the first British high commissioner, Sir Herbert Samuel, appointed a committee headed by Norman Bentwich, the attorney general, to consider the creation of a united Chief Rabbinate for the entire country. The committee recommended that a board of 71 electors, of whom two-thirds would be officiating rabbis and one-third laymen, elect a Chief Rabbinate Council for Palestine. This body would consist of Sephardi and Ashkenazi chief rabbis as joint presidents, three Sephardi and three Ashkenazi rabbis as members, and three laymen in an advisory capacity. The Rabbinate would function both as a court of first instance and as a court of appeal. A committee met early in 1921 to arrange the election. It drew up a list of 88 officiating rabbis (59 of them from Jerusalem) and 34 laymen. Later that year, the electors assembled in Jerusalem under the presidency of R. Yehudah Leib Fishman (Maimon[3]). After prolonged discussion, particularly over the proposal for lay counsellors, the elections took place on February 23, and the council was elected, with R. Kook and R. Ya'akov Meir as chief rabbis. (The Sephardi chief rabbi retained the title of *rishon le-Zion*.) The government immediately recognized the council and any *bet din* sanctioned by it as "the sole authorities in matters of Jewish Law" and undertook to execute through the civil courts judgments given by its *bet din*. The appointment of *ḥakham bashi* was declared to have lapsed. In 1922 the jurisdiction of the Chief Rabbinate was defined by the Order-in-Council. Section 53 of the order stipulated: "The Rabbinical Courts of the Jewish Community shall have: (a) exclusive jurisdiction in matters of marriage and divorce, alimony and confirmation of wills of members of their community other than foreigners ... (b) Jurisdiction in any other matter of personal status of such persons, where all the parties to the action consent to their jurisdiction. (c) Exclusive jurisdiction over any case as to the constitution or internal administration of a Wakf or

[3] Rabbi and leader of religious Zionism (1875–1962)

religious endowment constituted before the Rabbinical Courts according to Jewish Law." In 1928, when the government finally approved the Regulations of the Jewish Community Keneset Yisrael, the Chief Rabbinate Council was recognized by it as the supreme religious body of the Jewish community.

The Chief Rabbinate was not recognized by the religious zealots of Jerusalem. Nonreligious Jews set up their own Courts of Peace *(battei mishpat ha-shalom)*, which followed a combination of civil and Jewish law. Although the Mandatory authorities and their High Court of Justice tended to restrict the jurisdiction of the Rabbinate, it regulated a number of matters that had been neglected. It supervised, for example, compliance with the biblical precepts concerned with the cultivation of the soil, such as the separation of tithes *(ma'aser)* from agricultural produce, and the proper observance of the laws of *orlah* and *kilayim*. With the decline of the craft of the scribe in Eastern Europe, all manner of individuals in Jerusalem began to engage in the writing of scrolls of the law and the texts for phylacteries and *mezuzot*. By its certification stamp, the Rabbinate was able to assure purchasers that the articles were produced in conformity with the prescriptions of Jewish religious law. The Rabbinate also arranged for the immigration of some 3,000 rabbis from Europe above the regular immigration quota.

The Chief Rabbinate Council was enlarged by the co-option of a number of renowned religious scholars. The first incumbents were succeeded by Chief Rabbis Isaac Halevi Herzog (1936–59) and Ben-Zion Meir Ḥai Ouziel (1939–54). During their tenure, relations with the lay authorities were harmonious and fruitful. R. Herzog played a leading role in the relations between the Jewish population and the Mandatory government. He frequently appeared on behalf of the *yishuv* before the high commissioner and the various commissions appointed to investigate the situation in Palestine. Together with his colleague, R. Ouziel, he initiated cooperation between scientists and rabbis in seeking technological solutions to halakhic problems. He hailed the emergence of the new State of Israel as the beginning of the ultimate redemption.

Local Rabbinates. According to the regulations of Keneset Yisrael, the *battei din* and communal rabbis appointed by a local community and sanctioned by the Chief Rabbinate were recognized as official rabbis and served as the religious representatives of the community in its relations with the governmental district authorities. The local rabbinates served as courts of first instance and their offices worked harmoniously with the committees of the local communities. With the increase in the population of Jaffa and, later, in Tel Aviv, hundreds of synagogues, houses of study *(battei midrash)* and yeshivot were established and many district rabbis were appointed. *Battei din* with limited jurisdiction were set up to deal with divorce, *kashrut,* etc. The two local chief rabbis were R. Solomon Aronson and R. Ouziel. Rabbi Aronson was succeeded, on his death in 1935, by R. Moshe Avigdor Amiel, a leader of the World Mizrachi movement, and on his death in 1946 was succeeded by R. Isser Yehuda Unterman, and was followed in 1968 by R. Shlomo Goren, who was followed in 1973 by R. Yedidyah Frenkel. R. Ouziel was followed, on his appointment as joint chief rabbi of Palestine in 1939, by R. Moshe Toledano, a native of Tiberias, and was followed in 1968 by R. Ovadiah Yosef, who was followed by R. David Ha-Levi in 1973. In Haifa R. Yehoshua Kaniel, of Jerusalem, was appointed in 1922 to the *bet din* and later became the Ashkenazi chief rabbi of the city. Sephardi chief rabbis of Haifa were R. Eliahu Reine (1923–43), R. Nissim Ohanah (1943–66), and R. Yosef Mashash (1966–   ). In Jerusalem R. Zevi Pesah Frank served as Ashkenazi chief rabbi of the city (1936–1960). The Sephardi chief rabbis were R. Hizkiyyah Shabbetai, and Eliyahu Pardes (1961–1972).

The Kehillot (Community Councils). A single community council had served both the Ashkenazim and Sephardim of Jaffa and continued to function for both towns when Tel   13

Aviv was founded. At first it drew its income from *shehitah* fees; only in 1919 was a small, direct tax levied, yielding LP500–1,000 per annum from 1919 to 1925. A joint council was elected in Haifa in 1908 and conducted its operations energetically from its inception. The other communities, however, lacked resources and could not control the local institutions or provide adequate communal services; for generations they had been accustomed to rely on outside support from the *halukkah* or other forms of financial aid. In Jerusalem the first community council was elected in 1918, and similar bodies came into being in Tiberias, Safed, and Hebron in 1919. It was only after the regulations governing the *kehillot* were finally approved by Keneset Yisrael in 1928 that the community councils began to increase their activities. They determined the number of rabbis to be appointed and set up their own *shehitah* boards, later called religious councils, which organized and supervised religious facilities and services: *shehitah*, synagogues, ritual immersion pools *(mikva'ot)*, interments, the separation of tithes from agricultural produce, etc. Where not less than three-quarters of the local population were Jewish, the municipal authority, according to an act of 1921, also performed the functions of the community council or *kehillah*.

Only in 1932, after protracted negotiations with the existing council in Jerusalem, did elections for a new council finally take place there. Several years had to pass before the Jerusalem community council embraced all public services: welfare, culture, education, etc.; its religious council was responsible for *shehitah, kashrut*, burials, and so forth. In 1929, the Va'ad Le'ummi, the executive organ of Keneset Yisrael, resolved that the community council of Tel Aviv and Jaffa should amalgamate with the Tel Aviv municipal council, which, as Tel Aviv was a totally Jewish city, could fulfill the functions of both bodies. The community council refused to accept the decision, however, and held its own elections in 1933. Its activities were limited **14** to religious services and in 1939 it was absorbed by the municipality. The community council in Haifa was founded in 1931. In Safed elections for the community council took place in 1932 and in Tiberias in 1934. The Jews of Hebron, who were evacuated after the Arab massacre of 1929, returned in 1931 and elected their community council, but were obliged to leave again in 1936 on account of Arab violence. By the beginning of the 1940s, community councils had been set up in Petaḥ Tikvah, Bene-Berak, Ramat Gan, Netanyah, Haderah, Reḥovot, and Bat Yam; in other localities, local committees were recognized as community councils, while in some places religious councils were also established.

Education and Settlement. In 1920 the Mizrachi combined its schools with some other religious ones under a supervisory committee headed by R. Ouziel. This religious network, which consisted of 15 primary schools and eight kindergartens, with 2,137 pupils (compared with 6,622 in the general schools), became a part of the Zionist school system with an inspector of its own, and, after prolonged negotiations, was granted autonomy within the system.

Yeshivah in a Bene-Berak synagogue, 1927. Courtesy J.N.F., Jerusalem. Photo Schweig.

The Mizrachi educational system grew rapidly: in 1928 it had 61 schools and 5,774 pupils. In 1948, there were 26,654 pupils in the Mizrachi trend—about one-fifth of the total; 7,253 in Agudat Israel schools; some 3,000 in those of the old *yishuv;* 2,000 in private schools; and 4,000 in yeshivot.

Modern secondary yeshivot were founded by the religious youth movements: Benei Akiva (the first at Kefar ha-Ro'eh in 1940); No'ar Mizrachi (the first at Pardes Ḥannah in 1945) and Ezra, the youth movement of Po'alei Agudat Israel.

Apart from the religious pioneering youth movements, which established collective and cooperative settlements, Ḥasidim from Poland arrived in the 1920s, during the Fourth Aliyah, and participated in the "return to the soil." Although they had never worked with their hands before, they stood up to their knees in the marshes, their caftans tucked in at the waist, devoting themselves with ḥasidic fervor to what they regarded as a sacred task: draining the swamps of the Holy Land. In 1924 they founded the first religious moshav, Kefar Ḥasidim, in the valley of Zebulun. Bene-Berak, near Tel Aviv, was founded in 1925 by another group of Ḥasidim from Poland. It was planned as a moshav, but in the course of time it became a city with a large religious majority and many yeshivot.

In the State of Israel. Religious Jewry—with the exception of the ultraorthodox Neturei Karta—played its full part in the struggle for statehood: yeshivah students fought with the Haganah and other underground organizations; bearded and sidelocked Jews helped to build the emergency "Burma road" to besieged Jerusalem in 1948. Agudat Israel, which had refused to join the institutions of Keneset Yisrael and the Jewish Agency, was represented in the provisional council of state and the provisional government. The mass immigration of the first few years contained a high proportion of religious Jews—especially from the oriental countries. Hundreds of synagogues were built, and refugee scholars from Europe set up yeshivot bearing the names and continuing the traditions of those destroyed by the Nazis.

At the first elections to the Knesset, the four religious parties—Mizrachi, Ha-Po'el ha-Mizrachi, Agudat Israel, and Po'alei Agudat Israel—formed the United Religious Front, which joined the first coalition government after its demands on religious questions, such as the deferment of yeshivah students and the exemption of religious girls from the military service, had been met.

Article 2 of the government's statement of Basic Principles, presented to the Knesset on March 8, 1949, reads:

> The state will provide for the public religious needs of its inhabitants but will prevent coercion in matters of religion. The Sabbath and the Jewish holy days will be fixed days of rest in the State of Israel. The right of non-Jews to their Sabbath and days of rest will be safeguarded.

These principles were restated and rephrased by later governments. From 1959 they were supplemented by the obligation to "guarantee religious education to all children whose parents so desire" and to "maintain the status quo in the state in religious matters," thus confirming an unwritten agreement which had been in force since the establishment of independence.

One of the reasons why the Knesset did not immediately proceed to enact a comprehensive written constitution was the opposition of the religious parties. In the debate on the subject in 1950, they objected to a constitution which did not clearly express the religious character of the Jewish people; the Agudat Israel representatives declared that "Israel's Torah is her constitution" and no other was needed.

Ministry of Religious Affairs. The powers of the Mandatory high commisioner in matters of religion were transferred to the minister of religious affairs, who was responsible for the administrative aspects of the Chief Rabbinate and the rabbinical courts, the religious councils and religious committees, and the appointment and maintenance of local rabbis. The ministry deals with **17** *kashrut,* yeshivot, synagogues, *mikva'ot,* the supervision of burials, and the provision of ritual appurtenances and sacred books. It is responsible for the arrangements at the Western Wall and supervises the activities of the Sabbath Observance Council and Keren Yaldenu ("Our Child's Fund"), which counteracts the use of material inducements by missionary organizations. The ministry also provides religious services for Karaites and Samaritans, Muslims, Christians, and Druze.

Rabbinical Courts and the Chief Rabbinate. In 1953 the Knesset passed the Rabbinical Courts Jurisdiction (Marriage and Divorce) Law, which gave the Chief Rabbinate and the religious courts sanctioned by it exclusive jurisdiction of all matrimonial cases, including alimony and support of children, for all Jewish residents, including foreign nationals. Jews may marry only by the traditional ceremony *(huppah ve-kiddushin)* after the marriage has been duly registered with the rabbinate, and only rabbis approved by the Chief Rabbinate may conduct marriage ceremonies. Rabbinical courts also have jurisdiction in matters of trusteeship, confirmation of wills, etc., where the parties involved accept their authority. Attempts have been made to legalize civil marriages by appeals to the High Court of Justice, and some people get around the law by civil marriage abroad (particularly in nearby Cyprus). A certain status has, however, been accorded by law to "common law wives." Rabbinical judges *(dayyanim),* who have the same status as judges of district courts, are appointed by the president of the state on the recommendation of a special committee and take the oath of allegiance in his presence (see below p. 98).

Sephardi Chief Rabbi Ouziel died in 1954, and in the same year the minister of religious affairs promulgated new regulations for the election of the chief rabbis and the Chief Rabbinical Council. Rabbi Yiẓḥak Nissim was elected *rishon le-Zion* and Sephardi chief rabbi for a five-year term in 1955. On the death in 1959 of Ashkenazi Chief Rabbi Herzog and the approaching end of Chief Rabbi Nissim's term of office, arrangements had to be made for new elections. After a lengthy controversy over the composition of the election arrangements' committee and of the electoral college, new regulations were issued by the minister of religious affairs in 1963, increasing the number of electors from 75 to 125. Rabbi Nissim was reelected and R. Isser Yehudah Unterman was elected Ashkenazi chief rabbi. In 1972 Rabbi Shlomo Goren was elected Askenazi chief rabbi and Rabbi Ovadiah Yosef was elected *Rishon le-Zion* and Sephardi chief rabbi.

The Chief Rabbinical Council has departments for *kashrut,* supervision of scribes (*soferim*), and committees for marriage licenses; confirmation of rabbinical ordination (*semikhah*); precepts specific to the Holy Land; and responsa on matters of *halakhah.* The chief rabbis preside over the *Bet Din Gadol* (Rabbinical Supreme Court), which hears appeals from decisions of the district rabbinical courts in Jerusalem, Tel Aviv, Haifa, Petaḥ Tikvah, Reḥovot, Tiberias, Safed, Beersheba, and Ashdod-Ashkelon. Regulations governing the election of local rabbis were issued by the minister of religious affairs in 1966.

Religious Councils. Under the Religious Services Budget Law (1949), which was given its final form in 1967, every local authority is required to appoint a religious council consisting of religious individuals that will provide all public religious facilities for the local population. The composition of each religious council must be ratified by the minister of religious affairs. Forty-five percent of the members are nominated by the minister, 45% by the local authority, and 10% by the local rabbinate. Any deficits in the operation of the religious council are covered by the local authority (two-thirds) and the government (one-third). In 1972, 186 such councils were in existence.

Education. Under the "trend" system, which was incorporated in the Compulsory Education Law of 1949, the state took over the responsibility for providing religious education at the option of the parents. At the beginning of the year, the Agudat Israel network had been recognized as **19** a fourth trend, so that there was now a choice of two types of religious school—Mizrachi and Agudat Israel (in addition to *talmud torah* and other schools outside the state system)—as alternatives to the general and labor trends. To cater to the numerous religious families among the new immigrants, especially from the Muslim countries, a religious subtrend (Reshet Dati) of the labor network was developed by Ha-Oved ha-Dati, but was frowned on by the religious parties. There was considerable difficulty in implementing the parents' rights to choose between the four trends in the immigrants' camps, particularly among the newcomers from Yemen and the other oriental countries who could not be expected to understand the differences between the various types of school. Besides, the Mizrachi and Agudat Israel argued that the Reshet Dati was being elevated to the status of a fifth, unauthorized, trend. At first it was agreed, as a compromise, that the Ministry of

Yemenite children in a Jerusalem *ḥeder,* 1950. Courtesy Jewish Agency, Jerusalem.

Education and Culture should run religious classes for the Yemenites, while in the other camps the parents would choose between religious and general classes, but the agreement broke down when the minister of education and culture, David Remez,[4] refused to apply it to the *ma'barot* (transitional settlements). The controversy led to a cabinet crisis in February 1951 and a premature general election.

The problem was solved by the passing of the State Education Law (1953), which abolished the trend system and instituted two types of schools, state and state religious, both under the control of the ministry. The Agudat Israel system remained independent. By this time, the Mizrachi trend had more than doubled in size, with almost 55,000 pupils. It became the nucleus of the state religious system, which was also joined by the schools of the Reshet Dati and a few of the Agudat Israel ones. The law provided that the system should have no connection with any party, communal, or other nongovernmental body and that the schools should be religious in their curriculum and way of life. An autonomous wing for state religious education was established in the ministry with power to supervise the religious aspects of the schools' work and ensure that teachers, inspectors, and headmasters were satisfactory from the religious point of view. Defining the goals and attitudes of state religious education, a brochure published by the ministry stated in 1953:

> In Israel a religious kindergarten, primary school or secondary school is an institution which aims at the religious personality. It does all the work which a kindergarten or an elementary school has to do in general, but does it in such a manner, with modes of presentation and interpretation of common subject matter, and with classroom and school life organized in such a way, that the pupil may be expected to grow into maturity imbued with ideas, principles and values that mark him as an observer, in deed and in creed, of the Jewish religion.

[4] Labor leader in Erez Israel (1886–1951)

In 1972–73 the primary schools of the state religious system had 92,588 pupils, over 25% of the total in Jewish schools.

More intense religious study is pursued in 28 yeshivah high schools, where students spend the majority of their day in the study of Talmud and also study secular subjects for the matriculation examination; 15 vocational and agricultural yeshivah high schools; and four schools for girls in the Benei Akiva movement.

Hundreds of yeshivot have been established: *yeshivot ketannot,* for students aged 14–15; yeshivah high schools, described above; *yeshivot gedolot* (for those aged 18–25); and *kolelim,* for married men, some of which give training for *dayyanim* in rabbinical courts, while others encourage research in specific fields. In 1972/73, there were 64 *yeshivot ketannot,* with less than 4,000 students; 28 yeshivah high schools, with 4,121 students; 15 vocational and agricultural yeshivot, with 2,793 students; 70 *yeshivot gedolot* with 7,040 students; and 175 *kolelim,* with 4,383 students—a total of about 22,000 students, including 1,000 from abroad. In 1972 the Ministry of Religious Affairs allocated IL 7,900,000 toward the maintenance of yeshivot. After the Six-Day War, new yeshivot were established in the Old City of Jerusalem, Kefar Ezyon, and Hebron.

In Bar-Ilan University students are required, in addition to the regular curriculum, to take a number of courses in Judaic studies and to conform to religious standards. The Jerusalem College for Women, established in 1964, provides a three-year course, and its graduates are recognized as having the equivalent of a B.A. degree for high school teaching purposes. The type and intensity of the religious training is similar to that of the yeshivah. There is also a religious technical college in Jerusalem, which provides intensive talmudic training in addition to the study of technical subjects.

Agudat Israel schools, which preferred to stay out of the state system and established its Ḥinnukh Azma'i (Independent Education), are recognized and supervised (though not

Ashkenazi chief rabbi Issar Yehudah Unterman lecturing at the dedication of the *bet ha-midrash* at the Yeshivat ha-Kotel in the Old City of Jerusalem, 1970. Courtesy Yeshivat ha-Kotel, Jerusalem. Photo K. Weiss, Jerusalem.

Boys learning to put on *tefillin* at the Kefar Ḥabad annual bar mitzvah celebration for Six-Day War orphans. Photo Isaac Freidin, Tel Aviv.

controlled) by the state and 85% of their costs are met from the state budget. The system opened in 1953/54 with an enrollment of 16,000; in 1972/73 it had 179 schools with over 25,000 pupils. Religious education, in the aggregate, covers some 35% of the pupils in Jewish schools.

Ḥasidic Settlement. Soon after Israel became independent, the rabbi of Lubavitch, the head of the Ḥabad Ḥasidim, who lived in the United States, urged some of his followers, originally from the Soviet Union, to settle in Israel. They founded Kefar Ḥabad, the Lydda Yeshivah, and a number of other institutions. Other ḥasidic leaders have followed in their wake. R. Yekutiel Halberstam, the rabbi of Klausenburg, founded the Kiryat Zanz quarter in Netanyah and a quarter in Jerusalem; the rabbi of Vizh'nitz founded a quarter in Bene-Berak and the rabbi of Bobova one in Bat Yam; the rabbi of Sasov established Kiryat Yismaḥ Moshe and Rabbi Shemuel Ehrenfeld, Kiryat Mattersdorf. Even the rabbi of Satmar, the leader of the Neturei Karta, an inveterate opponent of the "Zionist state," built quarters for his followers in Jerusalem and Bene-Berak.

Various Religious Trends. A number of groups, some of them loosely organized, have tried to work out the implications of modern conditions, particularly the revival of statehood, in the sphere of Jewish religious thought and practice. They have expressed their views on public platforms, in the press, and in periodicals devoted to religious study and thought. Some religious intellectuals, like Yeshayahu Leibowitz and Ernst Simon have maintained that the *halakhah* was created to meet the needs of Diaspora life and must therefore be adapted to the new exigencies and opportunities of Jewish sovereignty. The Movement for Torah Judaism, headed by Ephraim Urbach, has worked for the regeneration of religious life on a nonparty basis within the framework of the *halakhah.* Both groups had some influence in academic circles, especially among student groups like the Yavneh Association, which sought to

harmonize the achievements of science and technology with

Jewish religious principles and called on the rabbinate to march with the times. There were also various unattached scholars and thinkers, like Samuel Hugo Bergmann and Dov Sadan, who tried to establish religious ideas on philosophical, scientific, or mystical foundations.

The radio helps to increase interest in the Jewish religious heritage by regular daily Bible readings and commentaries, talks on the Talmud and the Midrash, and discussions on religious problems; there are weekly television programs for the end of the Sabbath and special features for festivals. The Bible Study Association holds well-attended conventions, arranges study groups, and issues publications in which religious and nonreligious scholars combine to cast light on the Scriptures. There are various schemes to encourage and facilitate systematic study of a daily page of Talmud or paragraph of the Mishnah by disseminating, in pamphlet form, selections from talmudic material and rabbinic commentaries. Religious ceremonials associated with family occasions, such as circumcision, bar mitzvah, marriage, and interment and mourning, are observed by the vast majority, even of those who would not define themselves as "religious."

Controversy Over Religious Questions. Though the nonobservant majority regard religion as a matter for the conscience of the individual and resent administrative or legislative restrictions imposed on religious grounds, no *Kulturkampf* has developed. The observant do, however, manifest some tendency to isolation, some of them concentrating in predominantly religious areas. Controversies have flared up from time to time over the application of religious laws and principles to matters in the public domain. Examples are: complaints of inadequate provision for religious education, partially resolved by the appointment of a National Religious Party member as deputy minister of education and culture; licenses for Sabbath work in factories; road traffic on the Sabbath, particularly in the vicinity of religious quarters in Jerusalem; *kashrut,* e.g., the controversy over the proposal to install two kitchens, one non-*kasher,* in the Zim liner *Shalom;* autopsies, which are sanctioned by the more Orthodox only in rare cases and which, in the view of moderate religious circles, are performed too frequently and with inadequate safeguards; the refusal of the rabbinate to recognize divorces issued by Conservative rabbis in America; the Chief Rabbinate's directives on marriages with members of the Bene Israel community from India; and the inauguration of television broadcasts on the Sabbath.

The most prolonged controversy has been that over the question of "Who is a Jew?" i.e., how should Jewish "nationality" *(le'om)* be defined for the purpose of the population register? The argument led to a cabinet crisis in 1958 and broke out again in 1970 after the Supreme Court ruled by a majority that a Jewish father, married to a non-Jew, was entitled to have his children registered as Jews "by nationality." The Knesset thereupon passed a law providing that only persons recognized as Jews by the *halqkhah* (i.e., children of a Jewish mother or those converted to Judaism) may be registered as Jews by nationality, but amended the Law of Return to extend the privilege of automatic citizenship to the non-Jewish spouses and close relatives of Jewish immigrants. The controversy was reopened in mid-1970, however, over the recognition of conversions to Judaism performed by Reform and other rabbis not recognized by the Chief Rabbinate.

The Six-Day War and its aftermath have intensified the feelings of the Orthodox. The Western Wall draws worshipers at all hours of the day and night, and the crowds swell to tens of thousands on outstanding dates in the Jewish religious calendar. Orthodox Jews have been in the forefront of the establishment of yeshivot and synagogues in the Old City of Jerusalem, the resettlement of the Ezyon area, and the reestablishment of a Jewish community in Hebron.

SABBATH AND JEWISH HOLIDAYS IN MODERN ISRAEL. The outstanding feature of the Jewish Sabbath and festivals in Israel is their public character. Even before the establishment of the State of Israel, shops, offices, factories, and most restaurants in Jewish towns and areas were closed; most public transport was suspended and there was a pervading atmosphere of calm and repose. In Tel Aviv the Oneg Shabbat ("Joy of the Sabbath") meetings, founded by H. N. Bialik, drew large audiences. Observance was no longer, as in the Diaspora, hampered by the influence of the environment, but open and unrestrained.

In the State of Israel this trend became even more explicit. There is a virtual standstill in labor and trade on Sabbath and holy days: no newspapers are published; bus transportation is mostly suspended; no trains run; harbors and airports are inoperative; government offices and places of amusement are closed. Synagogues are full of worshipers and crowds stroll at their leisure in the streets and gardens. On the other hand, there are many taxis and private cars on the road; the television and radio operate; football and other matches are watched by large crowds of enthusiasts; privately organized trips by bus and truck take thousands of holidaymakers to the beach and country-side.

Some traditions observed in the Diaspora by only the most conscientious, however, are part and parcel of the national scene in Israel. Thus on the Day of Atonement broadcasting stops and there is virtually no vehicle to be seen in the streets. The traditional booths are seen everywhere at the Feast of Sukkot—in the courtyards or on the balconies or roofs, of even non-religious homes. On Simhat Torah and the following evening, the Scrolls of the Law are carried in procession through the streets by dancing and singing worshipers. Mass pilgrimages to Jerusalem, especially, since 1967, to the Western Wall, have become a traditional feature at Passover, Shavuot, and Sukkot, the pilgrim festivals of ancient times. On Hanukkah, the Feast of Lights, eight-branched candelabra blaze over public institutions and glow in every home. Young torch-bearers carry the light from the birthplace of the Maccabees in Modi'im to the president's residence in Jerusalem. **27**

Building a *sukkah* in Tel Aviv. 1959. Courtesy Government Press Office, Tel Aviv.

Simḥat Torah procession with Scrolls of the Law near the Tower of David in Jerusalem, 1967. Photo K. Weiss, Jerusalem.

The Western Wall at night, 1968. Courtesy Government
Press Office, Tel Aviv.

Tel Aviv nursery-school children celebrating Tu bi- Shevat
(the New Year of Trees). Courtesy Government Press
Office, Tel Aviv.

At dusk on the eve of the fast of the Ninth of Av restaurants, cafés, kiosks, and places of entertainment shut down to mark the anniversary of the destruction of the First and Second Temple. Tens of thousands walk to the Western Wall to chant the *kinot* ("dirges").

Minor festivals hardly observed in the Diaspora have been revived; they include Tu bi-Shevat, the New Year of Trees, on which thousands of trees are planted, and Lag ba-Omer, on which tens of thousands assemble in Meron, the traditional resting-place of R. Simeon b. Yoḥai, and bonfires lit by youngsters all over the country illuminate the skies at night. During the Purim holiday brightly costumed children parade the streets and transform it into a kind of popular carnival. Efforts have been made to evolve ways of celebrating Yom ha-Aẓma'ut (Independence Day) on Jewish traditional lines: special synagogue services are held, and several collections of prayers and songs

Purim *Adloyada* parade in Tel Aviv, 1968. Photo Werner Braun, Jerusalem.

have been published for the purpose. However, usages for converting the day into a full religious festival have not yet been universally accepted.

Public Services. Vital public services and utilities, such as power stations, water-pumping installations, telephone exchanges, and police services, continue to function on the Sabbath. Religious leaders and members of the Association of Religious Scientists are seeking technical ways and means of avoiding violation of the Sabbath. Some religious kibbutzim have developed automatic irrigation systems and milking machines for the purpose. The idea of using non-Jewish labor on the Sabbath has evoked much discussion and met with considerable opposition. In many instances, the principle of *pikku'ah nefesh* ("saving of human life"), which permits work on the Sabbath, has been applied; thus the supply of electric power and water to hospitals enables their use *post factum* in private homes. One extreme religious group does not, however, take advantage of this provision for non-urgent purposes.

In the Army. Rules for the observance of the Sabbath and festivals, as worked out by the chief chaplaincy of the Israel Defense Forces, are laid down in the standing orders of the general staff. They take into account the need for the army to be permanently alerted against potential attack. On Sabbaths and festivals all work ceases, except for duties which are essential for security. Leave is so timed that no soldier need travel on the Sabbath on his way home or on returning to his base. The chaplaincy, headed by Rabbi Shlomo Goren, has produced a unified prayer book for Ashkenazim and Sephardim, and deals with the elucidation of the religious law to meet every situation or eventuality. For example, on Rosh Ha-Shanah those in positions near the enemy lines are exempt from the injunction to listen to the sound of the *shofar* if there is a danger that the enemy may hear it. During actual fighting on the Day of Atonement a soldier in battle must break his fast as soon as he feels that hunger is affecting his fighting capacity; in hot areas, like the Arabah, he must drink water. **31**

On Sukkot those in outlying posts near enemy lines are exempt from the duty of dwelling in a *sukkah* by day and night. On Ḥanukkah soldiers having no candles or suitable oil may light the *menorah* with rifle or lubricating oil.

Excerpt from a mimeographed *Haggadah*, Kibbutz Sasa, 1949. The entire book was rewritten to make it meaningful to its first settlers, most of whom were American. Jerusalem,
32 B. M. Ansbacher Collection.

New Patterns. In the course of time new patterns of festival observance have emerged in the collective agricultural settlements, both religious and secular. In the nonreligious villages they have been almost entirely transformed into nature festivals, and religious aspects are given a secular interpretation, while the religious settlements have added modern nuances to old traditions. In the secular kibbutzim, the reaping of the *omer* is celebrated on the second day of Passover and the bringing of the *bikkurim* ("firstfruits") is observed on the eve of Shavuot. The religious settlements, however, feared that a revival of ancient custom in this form might be regarded as a transgression of the *halakhah,* which forbids "the bringing of the offering outside the precincts of the Temple area." In all kibbutzim, both religious and nonreligious, the *seder* is celebrated as a large communal festivity, but while the religious kibbutzim keep to the traditional text of the *Haggadah,* the nonreligious ones have introduced alterations in the traditional text and added modern literature and pieces of a topical nature.

The Legal Framework. Under the British Mandate, attempts to promulgate a countrywide Sabbath law applying to the Jewish population were unsuccessful. Consequently the religious representatives in the Jewish townships and municipalities pressed for local legislation. In 1948, on the eve of the establishment of the state, such bylaws, varying from one place to another, were in force in 42 towns and localities. One of the first legislative acts of the Provisional State Council after independence was aimed at safeguarding the social aspect of Sabbath and festivals throughout the country. This was the Days of Rest Ordinance of June 3, 1948, which prescribed the Sabbath and the Jewish festivals as regular days of rest, while assuring non-Jews of the right to observe their own Sabbath and festivals.

The Hours of Work and Rest Law of 1951 grants every employee at least 36 continuous hours of leisure each week. For Jews this weekly rest period coincides with the Sabbath, and a similar rest is prescribed on the Jewish festivals. This law, however, does not cover cafés, the self- **33** employed, or cooperative enterprises, including public transport. These are regulated by municipal ordinances, which are not uniform. While cafés are open on the Sabbath, for instance, in Tel Aviv, they are closed in Jerusalem. In both cities the buses do not operate, while in Haifa they run on a limited schedule. In some townships with a mainly religious population, certain streets or quarters are closed to all road transport on Sabbath and festivals. The Council for the Sabbath, which operates within the framework of the Ministry of Religious Affairs, and local groups endeavor to have the existing laws enforced, and to have appropriate bylaws introduced in new communities. They also conduct extensive educational activity and press for further legislation.

The law grants the minister of labor authority to permit work on the Sabbath in enterprises regarded as vital to national security or the economy, or installations like blast furnaces or cement kilns which require continuous operation. The issue of licenses to work on Sabbath is subject to approval by a committee consisting of the prime minister, the minister of religious affairs, and the minister of labor.

NON-ORTHODOX CONGREGATIONS. *Conservative Judaism.* The first Conservative congregation in Erez Israel, called Emet ve-Emunah was founded in 1937 in Jerusalem by newcomers from Germany and headed by Rabbi Kurt David Wilhelm, who was authorized to perform marriages by Chief Rabbi Kook. Rabbi Wilhelm was succeeded by R. Aharon Philipp (1948–70), who was also authorized. In 1970 there were also Conservative congregations in Ashkelon, Haifa, Netanyah, and Tel Aviv, of which the first two had recent arrivals from the United States as rabbis. These congregations were a part of the Conservative World Council of Synagogues forming a separate branch. The teaching arm of Conservative Judaism, the Jewish Theological Seminary of America, maintained a student center in Jerusalem and Conservative youth groups conducted summer educational programs in Israel.

At its convention in Jerusalem in 1970, the second to be

held in Israel, the World Council of Synagogues urged the Israel authorities to grant full recognition to Conservative rabbis in all spheres of religious life. The convention recognized the importance of "fostering a greater climate of understanding, awareness, and commitment among our communities toward the serious problems facing Israel" and resolved to encourage *aliyah,* visits by students, and other forms of direct contact with Israel.

Progressive Judaism or Reform Judaism. Progressive or Reform Judaism was introduced into Israel in 1957 on the initiative of the Israel Committee of the Central Conference of American Rabbis. After a visit by Rabbi Herbert Weiner, a founding committee was established in Jerusalem under the chairmanship of Shalom Ben-Chorin. The services were held first in an apartment and later in a public hall until, in 1962, the congregation moved into its own synagogue, the Har-El. Congregations were also established in Tel Aviv, Haifa, Ramat Gan, Kefar Shemaryahu, Nahariyyah, Upper Nazareth, Beersheba, and Natanyah, as well as a second congregation in Jerusalem at the Hebrew Union College. In 1959 the Progressive community joined the World Union for Progressive Judaism, which sent rabbis to serve it.

The Progressive congregations in Israel are organized in the Va'ad Arzi (National Board), which works with the Israel Committees of the World Union for Progressive Judaism and the Union of American Hebrew Congregations. Four full-time rabbis constitute Mo'eẓet ha-Rabbanim ha-Mitkaddemim—Maram (Council of Progressive Rabbis), which discusses policy on liturgy, *halakhah,* and public issues. The movement has published its own prayer book, the first issued by the Reform movement entirely in Hebrew, and a *maḥzor* for the High Holidays. The main differences between the services and the traditional ones are that men and women pray together and that congregational singing is accompanied on the organ. The Leo Baeck School in Haifa (founded in 1939), with 700 primary and 250 secondary pupils, and the Hebrew Union College Biblical and Archaeological School, Jerusalem, founded in 1963, are affiliated to the WUPJ.

The Progressive movement in Israel has no official status. Its rabbis are not entitled to perform weddings, grant divorces, or carry out conversions. The Biennial Conference of the WUPJ, held in Jerusalem in 1968, demanded "full and unreserved recognition of the religious rights of all Jews in Israel who are not Orthodox, and the complete and uncompromising accordance to them of all privileges, prerogatives and services presently enjoyed by the Orthodox Jewish Community of the Jewish State." As first steps the Conference urged that: 1) Progressive Jews in Israel be allowed to marry those registered in the Rabbinate as eligible for marriage; 2) anyone converted to Judaism by Reform or Liberal rabbis anywhere be recognized by Israel as Jews and admitted to Israel under the Law of Return; 3) Progressive congregations in Israel receive full support and aid from the Ministry of Religious Affairs. The amendments to the Law of Return and the Population Registry Law passed by the Knesset on March 10, 1970, which did not define the term "conversion," implicitly conceded the second claim in regard to conversions carried out abroad. The minister of justice stated subsequently, however, that in Israel the position was governed, in his view, by the Mandatory Ordinance of 1927, which required the consent of the Chief Rabbinate to conversions to Judaism.

Other Trends. Another non-orthodox manifestation in Israel's religious life is represented by the Jerusalem congregation *Mevakkeshei Derekh* (which is unaffiliated with any trend). This grew out of a series of national meetings (in 1962ff.) between city and kibbutz intellectuals who were trying to find a new way of expressing their religious beliefs in the context of the new situation emerging from the realities of the State of Israel, which they saw as a potential religious force in world Jewry and not only in Israel. The emphasis was not so much on *halakhah* as on Judaism as a communal force. Its prayer service represents the consensus of the group and is built on reading Torah and study.

2 MUSLIMS

At the end of 1972, there were about 358,600 Muslims in pre-1967 Israel, about 11% of the population, 610,000 in Judea and Samaria, and 390,000 in the Gaza Strip and Northern Sinai.

UNDER TURKISH RULE. Islam did not draw any distinction between "church" and state, for the latter had both political and religious functions. The Muslims of the Holy Land, therefore, saw no reason to organize as a community. They felt that they were the state, and the government should put their needs first. It was the non-Muslims who needed communal organizations recognized by the authorities and enjoying internal autonomy to protect their interests. The Muslims were almost all Sunnites, most of them, especially in the villages, belonging to the Shāfiʿī school, though the Shariʿa (Muslim religious) courts were conducted according to the Ḥanafī school, prevalent in the towns. Religious life in the countryside followed tradition, receiving inspiration and content from the mosques and the tombs of holy men. In some of the villages, especially the district of Samaria, renowned for its religious fervor, orders of zealots developed which maintained *zawāyā* (small prayer houses) as meeting places for their adherents. Traditional religious education was given in both town and village, the imam serving as teacher in addition to his other duties. These classes were replaced in the course of time by more modern schools, which were taken over by the British Mandatory government. The pilgrimage to Mecca was the aspiration of all, even the poor making great efforts to get there despite the expense and danger involved, and the return of a pilgrim was a major event. Sufi orders maintained *zawāyā* and *takāyā* (hostels) in Jerusalem, where lodgings were provided for pilgrims on their way to Mecca and bread and soup for the poor, drawing their revenues from waqf (religious trust) funds and contributions from the pilgrims. Such institutions were founded by immigrants from North Africa, India, Bukhara, and Afghanistan.

However, the charitable and educational institutions which the Egyptian rulers had founded in the Ayyubid[5] period, especially in Jerusalem around the Al-Aqṣā Mosque, were in a state of progressive decline. They depended for their maintenance on the waqf revenues, estimated to total 40,000 Turkish pounds, which the government sent to Constantinople instead of devoting them to the purposes for which they were destined. This was one of the grounds for the dissatisfaction expressed in the Arabic newspapers that started to appear after the revolt of the Young Turks in 1908. Articles were published denouncing the neglect of educational and religious establishments, which was said to have led to a religious and spiritual decline. The writers demanded that the government use the income from the charitable trusts for the maintenance of the institutions and the establishment of new ones, such as a college for religious studies and a vocational school for the children of the poor, aid for the distressed and indigent, and the preservation of the Muslim holy places, some of which were beginning to pass into Christian hands. Fears were expressed for the future of the younger generation, many of whom were being educated in schools run by foreigners, whose teachings were not compatible with Ottoman loyalty or the principles of Islam.

These demands fell upon deaf ears—Turkey was too preoccupied with her wars to pay attention to them. One new religious institution, al-Madrasa al-Ṣalāḥiyya, a train-

[5] Dynasty of sultans in Egypt and Syria (1171–1250)

ing college for religious functionaries, was opened in Jerusalem during World War I in order to counteract the influence of religious leaders in the service of the British, but was shut down when the war ended.

UNDER BRITISH RULE. The passage from four centuries of Ottoman rule to the rule of a Christian government did not, at first, present serious problems for the Muslims. The experienced officials of the British military administration, transferred from Egypt to deal with civilian affairs, did much for religious life. Festivals were celebrated with great splendor under the patronage of the British authorities; plans were prepared for the repair of the Al-Aqṣā Mosque, and the expenses of the annual pilgrimage to Nebi Mūsā (the reputed tomb of the Prophet Moses) were borne by the government. In 1921 the Palestine Administration set up the Muslim Higher Council, a secular body, which managed the religious and judicial affairs of the community, ran the charitable trusts, and was responsible for maintaining mosques. Subject to government approval, it appointed religious judges and functionaries, as well as inspectors and other officials. The Council did little, however, to further religious life. Its attempt, in 1922–23, to set up a secondary school in Jerusalem to train religious functionaries was a failure. The only institution of the kind was the al-Jazzār school in the mosque of that name in Acre.

During the period of British rule, however, nationalist trends, previously not in evidence, came into prominence, working in close alliance with religion. From its inception, the Muslim Higher Council introduced the religious element into the Arabs' political struggle against the Jews. Mass celebrations of Islamic festivals became political demonstrations, often ending in violence. The younger generation was inflamed by religious fanaticism and incited to attack the Jews. Delegations were sent to all Islamic countries to warn the faithful of the danger of Jewish domination over the Al-Aqṣā Mosque, the third in importance in the Muslim world. As a result of the efforts of the 39 mufti of Jerusalem, Hajj Amīm al-Husseini, a Muslim Congress was held in Jerusalem in 1931, which helped to weld Muslim solidarity while furthering the mufti's political ambitions.

The Council was widely criticized in the Muslim community for its commercial enterprises, the preferential treatment of the favored few, the neglect of the villages and their religious functionaries, and the failure to build new mosques and further post-primary education. After the Arab revolt of 1936–39 some of the council's members were dismissed and it passed under government control. Several groups and institutions freed themselves from its domination and there was a revival of interest in religious life and education. In Haifa, for example, the improving economic situation and the desire to compete with local Christian institutions stimulated the Muslims to establish their own charitable trusts and educational institutions. After World War II a number of societies and clubs were set up to intensify devotion to Islam and reform Muslim social life on the basis of Islamic principles. The Muslim Brotherhood, founded in Egypt, established a few branches in Palestine.

UNDER ISRAEL RULE. The end of the British Mandate saw the complete collapse of Muslim public life. Most of the religious leaders, who had played a prominent part in political activity, fled the country. The religious judiciary crumbled and the charitable trusts were abandoned. Great difficulty was experienced in finding replacements for religious judges and functionaries, especially in the towns, and the whole system of Shari'a courts had to be reconstructed, with the aid of Sheikh Tahir al-Tabarī, the only qadi who remained. For the first time in the history of the relations between Judaism and Islam, Jewish authorities had to be responsible for organizing Muslim religious life.

The Israel government, through the Ministry of Religious Affairs, took steps to restore the institutions of the Muslim community. Shari'a courts were set up in Jaffa, Acre, Haifa, Nazareth, and Ţayyiba (for the central region,

Ramadan prayers in the courtyard of the Al-Aqṣā Mosque, Jerusalem, 1965. The Dome of the Rock is in the background. Photo Elia, Jerusalem.

where Muslims are numerous) and religious functionaries appointed under the authority of the qadis to mosques in towns and villages. Muslim advisory commissions were set up in Jaffa, Ramleh, Lydda, Haifa, and Acre to look after holy places and promote religious and welfare services. The revenues of the waqf properties, which were administered by the Custodian of Absentee Property, were used to finance the work of the commissions in religious education, health, and welfare, as well as the repair of mosques and the erection of new ones. The management of the holy places was entrusted to the Muslim Department of the Ministry of Religious Affairs and the government assumed responsibility for the salaries of religious judges and functionaries. By a law of 1965, the Custodian of Absentee Property was empowered to release waqf properties, the fruits of which were destined for religious purposes, education, and welfare to committees of trustees, which replaced the advisory **41** commissions, appointed wherever there were waqf properties and Muslim communities.

The adaptation of Muslim life to the laws of the land was a relatively smooth process. There was understanding, on the whole, for the laws that made primary education compulsory for girls as well as boys, fixed the age of marriage for girls at 17, gave women equal rights, prohibited bigamy and regulated divorce. These were not found to be in conflict with Muslim doctrine; the Israel Supreme Court ruled, for example, that polygamy is not obligatory under Islam.

There were about 100 mosques in pre-1967 Israel, over 20 of which had been built after 1948—notably the Mosque of Peace in Nazareth, the first to be erected to serve the city's 16,000 Muslims. Many mosques were restored with the government's assistance: for example, it contributed over IL 200,000 to repair the mosque of al-Jazzār in Acre. Some 200 religious functionaries receive monthly government stipends. The five Shariʻa courts (the one at Jaffa also has authority over Jerusalem), exercise exclusive jurisdiction over members of the community in matters of personal status, such as marriage, divorce, and inheritance.

The Circassians, who were brought over by Sultan Abdu-l-Hamid II in the 19th century, live in two Galilee villages: Kafr Kamāʼ and Rīḥāniyya. There are some 600 members of the Aḥmadiyya sect in Kabābīr near Haifa; they conduct missionary activities. Acre is the center of the Shādhiliyya movement of Sufis, the foundersǀof which are buried in the sect's zāwiya in the town.

Religious life follows its traditional path, Fridays and the festivals of Islam being recognized as official holidays for Muslims. The government of Israel declared its readiness to facilitate pilgrimages to Mecca, but the Arab states refused to cooperate. The Arabic station of the Israel Broadcasting Authority broadcasts daily readings from the Koran, as well as prayers and sermons on Fridays and Muslim festivals. Religion is taught in primary and

post-primary schools; the teachers are specially trained and

Mosque in the Circassian village of Kafr Kamā', January, 1966. Courtesy Government Press Office, Tel Aviv.

religious textbooks compiled. The popular traditional festivities, such as the pilgrimages to the tombs of Sayyidunā Ali near Herzliyyah and Nabī Ṣāliḥ at Ramleh, have been revived. For the first time in the history of the Muslims in the Holy Land, a regular government publication is issued (by the Muslim Department of the Ministry of Religious Affairs) containing the decisions of the courts and views on major Muslim religious problems.

After the Six-Day War. The reunification of Jerusalem after the 1967 war enabled all Muslims in Israel, for the first time since 1948, to pray at the Al-Aqṣā Mosque, since previously, as Israelis, they could not cross the armistice lines. However, the qadis of the Shariʿa courts in East Jerusalem, who continued to receive their salaries from the Jordanian government and obeyed its political directives, remained unwilling to come to an arrangement with the Israel authorities on the regulation of matters of Muslim personal status. Other Muslim religious officials were paid by the waqf. The qadi of Jaffa, who had authority over Jerusalem, appointed four marriage registrars for the Muslims of the Holy City, who celebrated about 829 weddings for couples from Jerusalem up to 1972. The Shariʿa court in Jaffa also dealt with about 330 cases submitted by Jerusalem Muslims.

Muslim religious judges at a reception in the President's House, during the feast of al-Aḍḥā, Jerusalem, 1969. Seen left to right are Sheikh Ḥasan Amīn al-Ḥabash, qadi of the central region, Sheikh Ḥusnī al-Zuʿbī, qadi of Nazareth, Sheikh Amīn Qāsim Madlaj, qadi of Acre, and Sheikh Tawfīq Maḥmud ʿAsaliyya, qadi of Jaffa. Courtesy Ministry for Religious Affairs, Jerusalem. Photo K. Weiss, Jerusalem.

Leave-taking ceremony for pilgrims from Hebron setting
out for Mecca, 1970. Courtesy Aḥmad Shuwaykī Rifāʿī Hebron.

The situation in the Israel-administered areas of Samaria
and Judea, where the waqf administration looked after
mosque repairs and paid the religious functionaries, was
somewhat similar, while in the Gaza Strip the latter as well
as the qadis, received their stipends from the government of
Israel. In all the areas the Shariʿa courts continued to
function in the same way as under Jordanian or Egyptian
rule. The Israel authorities provided facilities for Muslims
from the administered areas to go on pilgrimage to Mecca,
but the Arab governments concerned still refused to extend
the privilege to Muslim citizens of Israel.

Despite the continued lack of religious leaders of stature, **45**

Islam serves as a general unifying factor in the Arab Muslim community. However, the practice of religion among them, as among other communities, is on the decline, particularly among the intellectuals and the city workers. This is due to the advance in education, the rise in the standard of living, the change in the status of women, the modernization of the towns and the countryside, and contact with new ways of life and thought, which have weakened the bonds of tradition and patriarchal discipline.

3 CHRISTIANS

In 1973 there were over 110,000 Christians, representing almost all the principal branches of Christendom, living under Israel rule, mainly in Jerusalem, Bethlehem, Ramallah, Nazareth and Galilee, Haifa, and Jaffa including almost 80,000—about 2.5% of the population in pre-1967 Israel. Most of them are town-dwellers and over 90% speak Arabic. Juridically, most belong to religious communities enjoying a large measure of autonomy in matters of personal status and led by patriarchs, who are both their high priests and ethnarchs. The "Community" is the ancient framework of the religious minorities in the Muslim world, but its roots go back to pre-Islamic times. The Ottoman government officially recognized a definite number of them, the so-called *millets.* This system was maintained by the British Mandatory power between 1918 and 1948 and still persists in Israel. In a schedule added in 1939 to the Palestine Order-in-Council of 1922, the religious communities are listed as follows: the Eastern (Orthodox), the Latin (Catholic), the Gregorian Armenian, the Armenian (Catholic), the Syrian (Catholic), the Chaldean (Uniate), the Greek (Catholic) Melkite, the Maronite, and the Syrian Orthodox. Neither the Copts and Ethiopians, nor the Anglicans and other Reformed Churches are mentioned in this list. The Church of England and the Evangelical Lutheran Church were subsequently granted official status by the government of Jordan, however, and the Evangelical Episcopal Church was recognized by the government of Israel in 1970.

Each community, as a rule, is headed by a patriarch

Candle store near the Church of the Holy Sepulcher, Jerusalem.
Photo Werner Braun, Jerusalem.

assisted by a synod or by an archbishop. The heads of the
recognized Churches appoint ecclesiastical courts of first
instance and courts of appeal. These courts have jurisdiction
in certain matters of personal status, such as marriage,
divorce, alimony, and confirmation of wills. In other
matters of personal status, such as legitimation and
adoption, guardianship, maintenance, and succession,
their jurisdiction is conditional upon the consent of the
interested parties.

The Christian religious communities have their headquarters in Jerusalem, where the most venerated Christian
sanctuary is the Church of the Holy Sepulcher. Equally
sacred to all Christian communities, it is controlled in

Pilgrims kneel at the Third Station of the Cross in the Via
Dolorosa on Good Friday. Photo Werner Braun, Jerusalem.

practice largely by the Greek Orthodox, Latin, and
Armenian patriarchates. The Syrians and the Copts have
small chapels within its precincts while the Ethiopians and
Anglicans have the use of chapels in its immediate
neighborhood. This situation is the "provisional" result of
centuries of struggle between the various churches over the
holy places. Since the question of the holy places has
never been solved, the position has been left, by agreement,
in *status quo ante*. Other holy places are to be found in
Nazareth and Bethlehem, and on the shores of the Sea of
Galilee.

THE (GREEK) ORTHODOX. The most ancient ecclesiastical
body in the Holy Land is the (Greek) Orthodox patriarch- **49**

ate of Jerusalem, which is probably the closest successor to the original Judeo-Christian community of St. James. A gentile, Greek-speaking, Christian community emerged in the city, then called Aelia Capitolina, before the middle of the second century, and gained importance in the days of Constantine (after the discovery of the holy places). In 451 Bishop Juvenal received the rank of patriarch. The Church of Jerusalem prospered in Byzantine times, decayed under the Arabs, was superseded by a Latin patriarchate during the Crusades, languished in the later Middle Ages, and recovered some strength under the Turks. At the beginning of the present century, however, it numbered a mere few

The Greek Orthodox patriarch enthroned in the Church of the Nativity in Bethlehem, Christmas, 1968. Photo Werner Braun, Jerusalem.

thousand, fighting for the preservation of Orthodoxy in the Holy Land. In 1972 there were some 39,000 Orthodox in Israel and the Israel-controlled territories.

The head of the church is the patriarch, who is assisted by a holy synod of 14 to 18 members. He is also supported by the Brotherhood of the Holy Sepulcher, made up of a hundred monks, almost all of Hellenic origin, which is the dominant factor in the life of the church, and from whose

Greek Orthodox monk at the Monastery of the Temptation on the Mount of the Forty (Quarantal), near Jericho. Courtesy Government Press Office, Tel Aviv.

ranks patriarchs, bishops, archimandrites, and other of-fice-bearers are elected. The Orthodox Church of Jerusalem is therefore an Arabic-speaking community led by an almost exclusively Greek-speaking hierarchy. The lower, married, clergy are Arabic-speaking. The Brotherhood enjoys important rights in the chief holy places, and is the sole owner of some. The patriarchate possesses 45 historic monasteries (some dating back to early Byzantine times) and numerous churches. The seat of the patriarch and the headquarters of the Brotherhood is the Convent of St. Constantine and St. Helena in Jerusalem, which also houses a library containing thousands of manuscripts, some going back to the tenth century.

Procession of Russian Orthodox priests leaving their church in the Russian Compound, Jerusalem. Courtesy Government
Press Office, Tel Aviv.

The Orthodox patriarchate of Jerusalem is the only autocephalous church in the country, all others being dependent in various degrees upon supreme hierarchs residing abroad, for example in Rome, Etchmiadzin (Soviet Armenia), Damascus, and Beirut. In Sinai there is a further autonomous (though not autocephalous) Orthodox church: founded in the third century as a missionary outpost, it is today a tiny monastic community, headed by an abbot with the title of archbishop. In 527 Justinian built a fortified monastery there, and in 566 a church in memory of his wife Theodora. In the ninth century, the monastery received the name of St. Catherine. It houses a famous library which includes numerous priceless manuscripts.

Jerusalem is also the seat of two Russian Orthodox missions. One of them represents the Moscow patriarchate; the other, the Russian Church Abroad. Both claim to be the legitimate successors of the ecclesiastic mission established by the Russian Government in the 19th century. The Moscow mission is in possession of the cathedral in Jerusalem and of a few churches in Jaffa, Haifa, Nazareth, and Tiberias, while the other is in charge of eight establishments, including the Church of St. Magdalene in Gethsemane. The mission of the Church Abroad, being out of communion with the patriarch of Moscow, is not recognized by the Orthodox patriarch of Jerusalem. A representative of the Rumanian patriarch is in charge of a church and a tiny community in Jerusalem.

THE NON-CHALCEDONIANS. These are the Churches which recognize only the dogmas defined by the first three ecumenical councils.

The Armenians. This group had 72 monasteries in the Holy Land in the seventh century, and its numbers increased considerably under the Arabs and Crusaders. As a result, much of Mount Zion became the property of the Armenian Church as early as the tenth century, and many splendid buildings were built there, e.g., the Church of St. Thoros. They prospered during the existence of the Armenian Kingdom of Cilicia, when they enjoyed the support of Armenian kings and princes and received numerous pilgrims. In 1311 (or perhaps 1281) their bishop was raised to the rank of patriarch. In later times they fared less well, losing all but six of their 72 monasteries, but they managed to maintain—against the Greek Orthodox—what they considered their rights in the main holy places. In Mandatory times (1918–48) they formed a prosperous community of some 5,000 souls, with their own churches, schools, and cultural institutions. Many have emigrated (to Soviet Armenia and elsewhere), and today they number over 2,500 in Israel-controlled territories.

The Armenian patriarchate is organized as the Monastic Brotherhood of St. James, composed of nine bishops, 32 archimandrites, and 70 monks. Only 36 serve in Israel; the remainder minister abroad. The head of the brotherhood is the patriarch, the leader of the church, president of all its

Armenians celebrating Christmas in the Church of the Nativity, Bethlehem, 1968. Photo Werner Braun, Jerusalem.

assemblies, and governor of church property, who also represents his community before the state. He is assisted by a holy synod, which derives its authority from the general assembly of the brotherhood. Supreme in Jerusalem, the partiarch is, however, to some extent dependent on the *Katholikós* of all the Armenians in Etchmiadzin (Soviet Armenia). The patriarchate of Jerusalem is of great significance to the entire Armenian nation on account of the holy places and the religious and cultural institutions of

Copts receiving the patriarch in their chapel in the Holy Sepulcher. Photo Werner Braun, Jerusalem.

which it is in charge. The Armenian patriarch enjoys a position similar to those of the Greek Orthodox and Latin patriarchs, with whom he shares the basilicas of the Holy Sepulcher in Jerusalem and of the Nativity in Bethlehem. He also holds in common with the Orthodox the Tomb of the Virgin on the outskirts of Jerusalem. The seat of the patriarchate is on Mount Zion, where the convent, the Cathedral of St. James with its historic treasures, the seminary, and the schools are situated. The library contains some 4,000 manuscripts, mostly of the Cilician period, including the oldest gospel in *erkataguir* characters, probably of the eighth century.

The Syrian Orthodox and Copts. The Syrians have had a bishop in Jerusalem since 1140, the Copts since 1236. The Syrian Orthodox (also called the Jacobites), numbering about 2,000 in what was formerly the whole of Jordan, are headed by an archbishop residing in the monastery of St. Mark. On Christmas, the Syrians and Copts celebrate at the Armenian altars in the Church of the Nativity. On other solemn occasions they officiate in their own tiny chapels in the Church of the Holy Sepulcher.

The Ethiopians. Although they owned a considerable number of chapels and altars in various holy places from the Middle Ages until the first part of the 16th century, the Ethiopians are today confined to the Deir al-Sultan on the roof of the subterranean chapel of St. Helena (in the Church of the Holy Sepulcher), a beautiful church and monastery (Debre Gennet) in western Jerusalem, and a chapel near the Jordan River.

THE CATHOLICS. The Catholic Church is represented in Israel by Latins and Uniates (Melkites, Maronites, Chaldeans, Syrian Catholics, and Armenian Catholics). Each community belongs to an independent jurisdiction, but all depend, severally, upon the Sacred Congregation of the Oriental Churches in Rome.

The Latins. The Latins number more than 24,000 Europeans, Arabs, and others. They are headed by a patriarch, under whose jurisdiction are those Latins

Rites in the Syrian Orthodox chapel in the Holy Sepulcher.
Photo Werner Braun, Jerusalem.

living in Transjordan and Cyprus. The Latin patriarchate
of Jerusalem, which was founded by the Crusaders in
1099, ceased to exist in 1291 but was reestablished in
1847/48. The patriarch is assisted by a coadjutor, two
auxiliary bishops and a chapter of canons. Seventy
diocesan clergy are in charge of 47 parishes distributed
over Israel, Jordan, and Cyprus. A patriarchal seminary
was founded in 1853.

Within the Latin community there are more than 45   **57**

religious orders and congregations. These include the Salesians with their orphanages and trade schools, the Brethren (Frères) with their colleges, the White Fathers and the Fathers of Beth Harram with their seminaries, the Trappists with their abbey at Latrun; the Benedictines with their abbey of the Dormition in Jerusalem, the Dominicans with the École Biblique, also in Jerusalem, the Carmelites, with their sanctuaries on Mt. Carmel, the Assumptionists, with their large organized pilgrimages, the Jesuits with their Pontifical Biblical Institute, and, most important, the Franciscans. There are 30 communities of women with more than 1,000 members and several hundred houses. These include the sisters of the Rosary (who are of local origin), the Sisters of St. Joseph, the Filles de la Charité, the Carmelite Sisters, the Sisters of Zion, and the Poor Clares.

Most of these religious "families" went to the Holy Land during the last 120 years, but the Franciscans had arrived centuries before the other orders. For more than 500 years (since 1333), their "Custody of the Holy Land" was the sole agency in charge of Catholic interests in Palestine and the Near East. They endeavored to regain rights of worship and possession in the major sanctuaries, rehabilitated abandoned shrines, attended to numberless pilgrims, and ministered to the tiny "Latin" communities that sprang up around their convents. In 1848, they surrendered some of their functions and prerogatives, but not the most important, to the restored patriarchate. With over 400 members drawn from 28 nations, they are still the guardians of the most important Catholic sanctuaries. While sharing, under the status quo, the Church of the Holy Sepulcher and the Grotto of the Nativity with the Orthodox and the Armenians, they hold in exclusive possession sacred sites in Nazareth, Cana, Capernaum, Tabor (all in Galilee), Gethsemane, Bethany, and Bethpage (all near Jerusalem), and Mt. Nebo. With worldwide Catholic aid, they have erected many churches and chapels, notably the monumental Basilica of the Annunciation in Nazareth, completed in 1967. Their Studium Biblicum is now a section of the theological faculty of the Pontifical University of St. Anthony in Rome. The numerous religious, cultural, educational, and welfare activities of the Latin Church in Israel, Jordan, and Cyprus are supervised by the apostolic delegate, representing the Holy See.

The Uniates (the Oriental churches in communion with Rome). The Uniates are represented in Israel by comparatively small communities, except for the strong Melkite community. The Maronites number about 3,500, for the most part near the Lebanese border; the Chaldeans and the Syrian and Armenian Catholics are a mere handful. Though all Uniate patriarchs reside in the Arab countries, their jurisdiction is recognized in Israel, where they are represented by patriarchal vicars in Jerusalem. None of the Uniate churches has rights in the principal Holy Places.

The Melkites are a most significant community. They are 26,500 strong: 23,500 in their diocese of Acre and Galilee and smaller numbers in Jerusalem and in the Israel-controlled territories. Under the guidance of their former archbishop, Georges Hakim (from 1967 Patriarch Maximus V of Antioch), they made great strides, increasing numerically, building numerous churches, establishing schools and seminaries, and integrating into the country's economic and social life. Arabic of speech, Byzantine of rite, and Catholic in church allegiance, they feel that they can play an important role in inter-church, and perhaps intercommunal, relations.

ANGLICANS AND PROTESTANTS. Reformed Christianity came to the Holy Land some 150 years ago. One of its aims was missionary work among Jews and Muslims, but most of its converts came from the (Greek) Orthodox. In 1841 an Anglican bishopric was established in Jerusalem in cooperation with Prussian Lutherans, the first incumbent being Michael Solomon Alexander, a convert from Judaism. The original accord between the English and the Germans broke down in 1881 and the bishopric was reconstituted in 1887 on a solely Anglican basis, the Lutherans carrying on independently.

Anglicanism prospered, especially in the Mandatory period, but by 1948 most of its English-speaking adherents left the country. Today the Evangelical Episcopal Church, some 2,000 strong, is overwhelmingly Arabic-speaking. The bishopric was raised to archiepiscopal rank in 1957, and the Anglican archbishop in Jerusalem presides over a synod composed of the bishops of Egypt and Libya, Sudan, Iran, and Jordan. In 1970 the church was recognized by the Israel government as a separate religious community. The Anglicans have no rights in the Church of the Holy Sepulcher, but they enjoy the privilege of occasionally celebrating in the nearby (Greek) Orthodox chapel of St. Abraham. The archbishop's own cathedral is the Collegiate Church of St. George in Jerusalem, consecrated in 1898.

German Lutherans established schools, hospices, and hospitals in the Holy Land, the best-known being the Augusta Victoria Hospice (now a hospital) on Mount Scopus, the Hospice of the Order of St. John in Jerusalem, the Talitha Kumi School at Bayt Jālā near Bethlehem, and the German Evangelical Institute for Archaeological Research in the Holy Land. Despite setbacks as a result of the two world wars, the Lutherans have reestablished themselves. Led by a *propst,* residing in the building of the Church of the Redeemer in the Muristan area of the Old City, they now form the Evangelical Lutheran Church numbering about 1,500, mostly Arab.

Non-German Lutheran institutions include the Swedish Theological Institute in Jerusalem, the Swedish school and hospital in Bethlehem, the Finnish Missionary School in Jerusalem, and the Scandinavian Seamen's Churches in Haifa and Ashdod. Reformed Christianity is also represented by a number of minor Protestant groups and agencies which, being mostly of foreign and recent origin, do not enjoy the status of official communities, although of course they have complete freedom of worship. These include Presbyterians, Baptists, Pentecostalists, the Society of Friends (Quakers), Adventists, and Brethren.

4 SAMARITANS

History. Until the middle of the 20th century it was customary to believe that the Samaritans originated from a mixture of the people living in Samaria and other peoples at the time of the conquest of Samaria by Assyria (722/1 B.C.E.). The biblical account in II Kings 17 had long been the decisive source for the formulation of historical accounts of Samaritan origins. Reconsideration of this passage, however, has led to more attention being paid to the chronicles of the Samaritans themselves. With the publication of Chronicle II (*Sefer ha-Yamim*), the fullest Samaritan version of their own history became available. Two types of information on Samaritan history are available: the chronicles, and a variety of non-Samaritan materials. According to the former, the Samaritans are the direct descendants of the Joseph tribes, Ephraim and Manasseh, and until the 17th century C.E. they possessed a high priesthood descending directly from Aaron through Eleazar and Phinehas. They claim to have continuously occupied their ancient territory in central Palestine and to have been at peace with the other Israelite tribes until the time when Eli disrupted the northern cult by moving from Shechem to Shiloh and attracting some northern Israelites to his new cult there. For the Samaritans, this was the "schism" par excellence.

It is not known as a matter of fact whether the priesthood in northern Israel survived the Assyrian conquest. Nor is there any evidence beyond Samaritan sources as to whether the Samaritans existed as a separate entity among the Samarians.

Little guidance is obtained from the name of the Samaritans. The Bible uses the name Shomronim (שֹׁמְרֹנִים) once, in II Kings 17:29, but this probably means Samarians rather than Samaritans. The Samaritans themselves do not use the name at all; they have long called themselves Shamerim (שַׁמֵרִים): i.e., "keepers" or "observers," of the truth = al ha-emet, both the short and long forms being in constant use in their chronicles. They take the name Shomronim to mean inhabitants of the town of Samaria built by Omri.

Chronicle II reports the reign of Xerxes, when the Judeans returned under Nehemiah. The dispute over the fortifying of Jerusalem is reported from the Samaritan viewpoint, according to which the Judeans were prevented from their purpose and the Samaritans, with royal authority, demolished all that had been built. The account contrasts with Josephus (Ant. 11:174–6), who credits the victory to Nehemiah. Another important question concerning the time and motives of the final schism between Jews and Samaritans is still under debate. One proposal reaches the conclusion that the conquest of Shechem by John Hyrcanus (in 128 B.C.E.) and the destruction of the Samaritan temple there brought about the final severance. Another proposal postpones the final breach to the times of the geonim.

The Chronicle II claims that an additional reason for this enmity was brought about by Ezra altering the script and contents of the Torah. There is no supporting evidence for this claim, however. According to Chronicle II Alexander the Great permitted the Samaritans to build a temple on Mount Gerizim (which was later destroyed by John Hycranus[6]). The Samaritans claim to have received from Alexander a deed of covenant to protect them. The Samaritan Chronicle II tells of the Samaritan success in winning over Ptolemy Philadelphus,[7] who was persuaded

---

[6] Ethnarch of Judea and high priest (135–104 B.C.E.)

[7] King of Egypt (285–246 B.C.E.)

to forbid pilgrimages to Jerusalem and prohibited the celebration of Jewish festivals there during his lifetime. According to the chronicles the Samaritan temple was destroyed by John Hyrcanus in 128 B.C.E. and rebuilt by the Romans as a reward for the aid given to them by the Samaritans during the Bar Kokhba[8] rebellion. The remainder of the period before Palestine became part of the Roman Empire is passed over quickly in the chronicles.

So far the Samaritan version of history has been parallel rather than similar to the Jewish version. From this point on the Samaritan chronicles are fuller and seem to be, in the main, quite different from the record of Josephus. The Romans, however, were not to distinguish between Jews and Samaritans, and Roman legislation was to be a heavy burden on both peoples in many respects. Throughout the chronicles, statements are made about the loss of Samaritan literature during times of persecution. The worst of these periods seems to have been during the rule of Hadrian[9] (and later of Commodus[10] and Severus[11]), when most of the literature kept in Shechem was destroyed. The high priest lists, however, were probably preserved.

During a long period of gradual christianization in Palestine, the Samaritans fared badly: there were continual attacks by Samaritans on Christians and Christians on Jews and Samaritans, and the holy places of Israel were taken over by the Christians. It is clear that thousands of Samaritans died in the fighting and that they tried to establish their own state.

According to the chronicles, many Samaritans fled eastward after 634, when the Muslims were victorious at Yarmuk. In 1137 Nablus seems to have undergone the catastrophe of further devastation and decimation of its inhabitants when the Saracens attacked it, and thereafter, until 1244, Muslims assumed rule of the Samarian capital.

---

[8] Leader of the revolt in Judea against Rome (132–135 C.E.)
[9] Roman emperor (117–138 C.E.)
[10] Roman emperor (180–192 C.E.)
[11] Roman emperor (193–211 C.E.)

The final destruction of the Crusader rule in Palestine by the Mamluks[12] (1291), who established their own hegemony over the country, did not bring about an improvement in the situation of the Samaritans. At the very beginning of their rule, the Mamluks plundered the Samaritan religious center in Shechem (Nablus) and turned it into a mosque, in addition to destroying all the other buildings there.

In addition to their foremost center in Shechem, the Samaritans also had an important center in Damascus from the 11th century. In the course of the 14th century the two centers achieved the height of their social and religious development.

During the same period the Samaritans had centers of secondary importance in Cairo and Gaza. Both these centers, as well as the one in Damascus, observed annual pilgrimages to Mt. Gerizim and the community centered in Shechem. The family of the high priests in Shechem functioned as the supreme institution for all the Samaritan centers.

With the beginning of the Ottoman conquest, the persecutions suffered by the Samaritans at the hands of their Muslim neighbors and local governors grew in strength and frequency. The small Samaritan community remained in existence until the beginning of the 18th century, when the surviving members joined the community in Shechem and Samaritan settlement in Egypt came to an end.

The most important event relating to the decrease in the size of the Samaritan community was the disappearance of the line of high priests descending from Aaron. Access to Mt. Gerizim was forbidden to the Samaritans by the Arabs, and they were forced to hold the Passover sacrifice on the eastern slope of the mountain.

At the beginning of the 19th century the Samaritans lived in a certain degree of comfort in Shechem, but once again the Muslims interfered and prevented them from ascending to the top of Mt. Gerizim for the Passover sacrifice. This prohibition was in effect until 1820, when

[12] Military class, ruled Egypt 1250–1517

the Samaritans were again allowed to go up the mountain due to the intervention of the British consulate with the Turks.

By the third decade of the 19th century, only the small community of Samaritans in Shechem remained. The Arabs of Shechem, incited by their religious teachers, cruelly persecuted the Samaritans. After the Samaritans turned to the Jewish community in Jerusalem, they received an authorization from the chief rabbi, Abraham Ḥayyim, that "the Samaritan people is a branch of the Jewish people that confesses to the truth of the Torah."

It can be seen with certainty that the replenishment of the Samaritan community in Shechem by the survivors of other Samaritan centers was the factor that allowed the Samaritans to survive the 400 years of Ottoman rule. Most of the Samaritans engaged in copying documents for scholars and tourist who visited Shechem at the beginning of the 20th century. The plague that broke out in Shechem at the time of the withdrawal of the Turkish army left the community with the smallest population in its history, 146 souls.

With the beginning of the British Mandatory administration in Palestine, the situation of the Samaritans improved. The family of Tsedaka from Shechem had moved to Jaffa and become acquainted with Izhak Ben-Zvi[13] already in 1907. Throughout his career in Palestine and the State of Israel, Ben-Zvi devoted attention to improving the situation of the Samaritans.

The Samaritan population doubled within a span of 30 years. With the establishment of the State of Israel (1948), the Samaritan community split into two centers: the first was in Shechem, under the government of the Hashemite Kingdom of Jordan; the second was in Israel, under the leadership of Japheth b. Abraham Tsedaka. As a result of Tsedaka's activities and Ben-Zvi's influence, in 1949 the Samaritans were recognized as citizens under the

---

[13] Second president of Israel (1884–1963)

Law of Return, a fact that contributed to the reunification of Samaritan families from Shechem and the growth of the Samaritan community scattered throughout Israel. In 1953 the Samaritans were allowed, for the first time, to cross the border to celebrate Passover with their brethren on Mt. Gerizim, and this privilege, attained through an agreement by the Israel-Jordan Mixed Armistice Commission, remained in effect until the Six-Day War (1967), when Shechem came under Israel rule. In 1954 all the Samaritans scattered throughout the State of Israel relocated in permanent living quarters in Ḥolon, and a unified Samaritan center was created in Israel. The Six-Day War ended the isolation of the two branches of the Samaritan community.

Religion and Customs. It is likely that the Samaritan creed in its earliest form was a simple statement of belief in God and in the Pentateuch. Belief in Moses as the sole prophet of God, so prominent a feature of Samaritanism, probably developed long before the Roman conquest of Palestine, and almost certainly belief in Mt. Gerizim as the one true sanctuary chosen by Israel's God was well established before Alexander the Great. Belief in the *taheb,* i.e., restorer (or according to some "returner"), as one who would restore all things prior to the last day, the cataclysm, the judgment, and finally paradise is undoubtedly the latest of the creedal tenets.

The doctrine of God is clear, simple, and mainly biblical. The absolute oneness of God is expressed on every hand.

A typical Samaritan feature is the prominence of their priesthood in the life of the community. The priests are the interpreters of the law and the keepers of the secret of the calendar, upon which the true observation of their festivals depends.

Since the Samaritans possessed only the Pentateuch as against the threefold Bible of Judaism and had no codified second law corresponding to the Mishnah, the outlines of their beliefs were easy to delineate. Moses was "the

A Samaritan priest, Jacob b. Uzzi ha-Kohen, with the most
ancient Samaritan Torah scroll, dating, according to
Samaritan tradition, from the 13th year of the settlement of
the Israelites in Canaan. Photo David Harris, Jerusalem.

prophet" to the Samaritans and Joshua alone of all the
other biblical prophets is held in high esteem, even called
king, because he is mentioned in the Pentateuch as the
servant of Moses, who was initiated by him to fill his
place. This last remark gives the clue to the development
of Samaritan doctrine, namely that no concept which had

no warrant in the Pentateuch could be regarded as valid. The Ten Commandments of the masoretic Bible are regarded as nine by the Samaritans, who have a tenth of their own (of considerable length) stipulating the prime sanctity of Mt. Gerizim.

On the practical side of religion, the Samaritans have developed their code of religious practice by direct interpretation of biblical laws. A *halakhah* came into being, though not in the same way as in Judaism. It often differs from the rabbinical *halakhah* by its stricter adherence to the letter of the law, as in the laws of Sabbath and festivals or marriage between close relatives. There was no systematic codification of the law, and the few extant Samaritan halakhic compendia are arranged very loosely.

Holidays and Festivals. THE SABBATH. The seventh day of the week serves as the basic rite for all Samaritan holidays and festivals. The Samaritan synagogue is always oriented toward Mt. Gerizim. The worshipers stand on rugs spread out on the floor, and before one enters the synagogue he must remove his shoes. In addition, the worshipers must have a head covering while praying.

The Samaritans do not light fires on the Sabbath or travel. They eat hot meals prepared beforehand only on the Sabbath eve, when they also kindle the lights that remain on throughout the Sabbath; neither do they leave the vicinity of their community.

THE FESTIVALS. The Samaritans celebrate seven *mo'adim*, four of which are called *mo'adim* and three *ḥaggim*. The *ḥaggim* are the pilgrimages ordered in the Torah, e.g., Ex. 23: 14–19. The first *mo'ed* is Passover, which falls on the 15th day of the first month. On the eve of the festival, the Samaritans carry out the ceremony of the sacrifice of the paschal lamb on Mt. Gerizim. The second *mo'ed* is the Festival of the Seventh Month, which is celebrated on the first day of the seventh month and is parallel to the Jewish holiday of Rosh ha-Shanah, except that it is celebrated for one day only. The third *mo'ed* is the Day of Atonement, which is celebrated on the tenth day

Samaritans celebrating the sacrifice of the paschal lamb on Mt. Gerizim. Courtesy Government Press Office, Tel Aviv.

of the seventh month from evening to evening. The fourth *mo'ed* is Shemini Aẓeret, which is celebrated on the 22nd day of the seventh month.

The first *ḥag* is Ḥag ha-Maẓẓot ("Feast of Unleavened Bread"), which is celebrated on the 21st day of the first month. The Samaritans make a pilgrimage to the top of Mt. Gerizim for the first time (in their cycle of *ḥaggim*). The second *ḥag* is the Festival of the Pentecost, which takes place on the day after the seventh Sabbath counted from the first Sabbath following Passover. As a result, it is traditional to celebrate this holiday on a Sunday. At this time the Samaritans make a pilgrimage for the second

Raising of the Torah scroll by a priest on the seventh day of
70 Passover. Courtesy Binyamin Tsedaka, Holon.

High priest, Avisha b. Phinehas (1941–60) and notables of the community during the prayer of the Passover sacrifice. Courtesy Binyamin Tsedaka, Ḥolon.

time. The third *ḥag* is Sukkot, which takes place on the 15th day of the seventh month, and the Samaritans make their third pilgrimage of the annual cycle. The Samaritans do not celebrate Purim or Hannukah because these holidays are not mentioned in the Pentateuch and were declared after the split between the Samaritans and the Jews. On the other hand, they celebrate the Independence Day of the State of Israel.

It should be noted that the Jews and the Samaritans rarely celebrate their holidays and festivals on the same days, as the determination of the beginning of the month and the intercalation of the years are made according to different calendar systems.

Religious Ceremonies. CIRCUMCISION· The Samaritans are obligated to circumcise their sons at the age of eight days, for any male who is not circumcised eight days after birth is not considered an "Israel Samaritan" (Genesis 17:14).

THE LAWS OF RITUAL IMPURITY AND PURITY. These laws are completely binding within the Samaritan community. During her menstrual period, for seven days, the woman is obliged to remain separated from her family, who must wait upon her and supply all her needs. A woman giving birth to a son is unclean 40 days, and if the child is a daughter she is unclean for 80 days, after which she purifies herself.

COMPLETION OF THE TORAH. The completion of the Torah sets the official seal upon the Samaritan's way of life in his tradition. In content it is reminiscent of the Jewish bar mitzvah ceremony, but the difference is fundamental. The Jewish bar mitzvah takes place at the age of 13, while the Samaritan's bar mitzvah is dependent upon his education and ability. Only after he has learned the whole Pentateuch can the ceremony of completing the Pentateuch be arranged for a boy by his father.

KIDDUSHIN. The proposal is the first of three stages in Samaritan marriage: kiddushin, erusin, nissu'in. The kiddushin ceremony takes place in the girl's home. The betrothal (erusin) usually takes place a short time after the kiddushin. Release from erusin requires a divorce. Marriage (nissu'in) is the final stage, the formal act whose purpose is to complete the betrothal. Rejoicing on these occasions is greater than at any joyful Samaritan ceremony. The bridegroom's family proclaims a week of rejoicing to begin the Sabbath before the wedding. The wedding takes place on the fourth day when the luminaries, symbolized by the bridegroom and the bride, were created. During the day the bridegroom takes a piece of parchment to one of the scholars among the priests and asks him to write the marriage contract (ketubbah).

Samaritan halakhah permits intermarriage with the Jewish community on authorization by the high priest after he is convinced that the convert will be fit to bear the brunt of observing Samaritan tradition.

Divorce occurs very rarely in the Samaritan community. There are three causes which are recognized by Samaritan *halakhah*: (1) abominable practices committed by either party, or by both together; (2) quarreling that makes the life of either party unbearable; (3) immorality, i.e., rumors or proofs that either party maintains extramarital relations. In each case the cause must be confirmed by two or three witnesses.

The Samaritans bury their dead in their cemetery on Mount Gerizim. They place the corpse in a coffin its head pointing in the direction opposite to the peak of Mt. Gerizim in order that his face should be toward the mountain. After the death, they read the Pentateuch all night long. On the next morning they wash the corpse. Anyone touching it becomes unclean and is obliged to bathe. They place the body in the coffin and carry it to the cemetery.

5 KARAITES

The meaning of the sect's name—Kara'im, Ba'alei ha-Mikra ("people of the Scriptures")—is assumed to imply the main characteristic of the sect, the recognition of the Scriptures as the sole and direct source of religious law, to the exclusion of the Oral Law. There is, however, another interpretation of the name Kara'im, defining it as "callers" or "propagandists." Since a religion based on revelation cannot tolerate the complete exclusion of tradition, either in principle or in practice, the Karaite demand for a return to Scripture should be taken as a theoretical watchword, directed not against all tradition, but specifically against the rabbinical tradition. As a matter of fact, the Karaites also developed a tradition of their own, described by them as *sevel ha-yerushah* ("yoke of inheritance"), consisting of doctrines and usages which, although not found in the Bible, were accepted as binding by the entire community.

The name "Karaites" was not applied until the ninth century; the principal component of the sect was originally known as "Ananites," from the name of its founder, Anan b. David. The sect appears to have come into being as the result of a combination of factors: the amalgamation of various heterodox trends in Babylonian-Persian Jewry; the tremendous religious, political, and economic fermentation in the entire East, resulting from the Arab conquests and the social and economic grievances of the poorer classes of Jewry, particularly those who had left the populous center of Babylonia and had migrated to the sparsely settled frontier provinces of the caliphate, where they were more or less independent of the Babylonian Jewish authorities.

As the Karaite movement did not recognize any single leader, it was not long before many sects arose in its midst, in opposition to the Ananites. In the ninth century and the beginning of the tenth, the Karaite movement was a conglomeration of various anti-Rabbanite heresies, some of which had sprung up after Anan's death. The many sects, which had come upon the Karaite scene after Anan, disappeared as fast as they had sprung up, without leaving any noticeable trace upon the movement. By their gradual self-liquidation, however, they prepared the ground for the consolidation of a well-defined, uniform doctrine which has subsisted to this very day as Karaism. In the tenth century, when Karaism was already fairly consolidated, the movement adopted an aggressive attitude, designed to spread its doctrine. This was also the golden age of Karaite literature (with most of the Karaite works of this period being written in Arabic). Karaite attempts to gain mass support for their beliefs among the Rabbanites (which, however, seem to have attracted only a few converts of no particular distinction) brought forth, on both sides, an apologetic and polemic literature.

Karaite missionary activity, while hardly successful, forced the Rabbanites to take note of their existence, and combat them. Karaite literature flourished in most of the areas under Muslim rule—in Egypt, North Africa and particularly in Erez Israel, in addition to Babylonia and Persia, where Karaism had come into being.

At that time Jerusalem was one of the outstanding spiritual centers of Karaism. At the end of the 11th century Karaite literary and scientific work in Erez Israel came to an abrupt end as the result of the First Crusade (1099). This seems to have marked the destruction of the Karaite community in Jerusalem. In 1642, according to the report of the Jewish traveler Samuel b. David, there were only 27 Karaites living in Jerusalem, and in the middle of the 18th century there were no Karaites at all. Karaite efforts, however, to maintain a representative group of pietists in the Holy City never ceased.

At the end of the 11th century, the center of Karaite intellectual activity shifted to Europe. In the second half of the 13th century, Karaism in the Byzantine Empire entered a new, though temporary, period of spiritual florescence.

It was during the 15th and 16th centuries that a rapprochement took place between the Karaite and Rabbanite Jews; Rabbanite scholars guided Karaites in the study of Jewish literature and secular sciences. In the 17th and 18th centuries, Karaite activity shifted to the Crimea and Lithuania, and Karaites in these areas assumed leadership of the sect. It was only at the end of the 18th century, when Russia conquered the Crimea, that a difference in status was made between Rabbanite Jews and Karaites under the law. In 1840 the Karaites were put on an equal footing with the Muslims, and were granted an independent church statute.

In 1932 there were approximately 2,000 Karaites outside Russia, in Poland (Halicz, Troki, Vilna,) Constantinople, Jerusalem, Cairo and Hit (on the Euphrates). The total number of Karaites in the world was approximately 12,000. On Jan. 9, 1939, the German Ministry of the Interior expressly stipulated that the Karaites did not belong to the Jewish religious community; their "racial psychology" was considered non-Jewish. This decision was subsequently applied to France. In Eastern Europe the Nazi *Einsatzgruppen* during World War II received orders to spare the Karaites, who enjoyed favorable treatment and were given positions of trust and authority with the German occupation authorities. In the Arab states, on the other hand, the persecution of Jews which followed upon the establishment of the State of Israel caused the Karaites (in Egypt, Iraq, and elsewhere) to settle in Israel, where they were welcomed and enabled to settle in compact groups, and were given government assistance in establishing themselves economically and in providing for their religious and educational needs. Their religious affairs are administered by nine precentors (*ḥazzanim*) and they have their own slaughterers and circumcisers, although Rabbanite practitioners are often called in. A number of religious books for their use have been published

Remains of the Karaite synagogue in the Old City of
Jerusalem, dedicated in 1864. Photo Werner Braun, Jerusalem.

recently, including a complete prayer book and Bashyazi's
Adderet Eliyahu. Although the Karaites are not recognized as a separate community, they have a separate *bet din*
to administer marriage and divorce. Both according to the
halakhah and their own laws, they are not permitted to in-
termarry with the rest of the Jewish population. Karaites
are liable to military service. Since Karaite law forbids being
counted in a census there are no exact figures as to the size

of the Karaite community. It is estimated that there are 10,000 Karaites in Israel most of whom lived in the following areas in 1973: Ramleh district 4,000, Ashdod 2,800, Ofakim, Beersheba, Rannen, Maẓliaḥ, Bat Yam, Acre, Kiryat Malakhi, Yavneh, Bet Shemesh, Mevasseret Zion, and Jerusalem.

In principle, the Bible is the sole source of Karaite creed and law. All religious precepts must derive directly from the Bible, based upon the literal meaning of the text, the customary use of the words and the context. Tradition is accepted, providing it is indispensable for the application of precepts contained in the text, for the clarification of ambiguities, or to make up for deficiencies in the concrete details of precepts: even so, however, its role remains restricted and subordinate. Certain rabbinic laws are accepted, not as valid components of the Oral Law transmitted by the Rabbanites, but as clarifying prescriptions, indicated in the text and reinforced by custom and tradition. For the rest, every scholar must study Scripture for himself, and if urged to do so by his own knowledge and conscience, alter earlier opinions. Thus, Karaite doctrine is characterized, on the one hand, by rigidity and immutability of tradition, and, on the other hand, by an absence of restrictions on individual understanding of the Scriptures.

Apart from its fundamental stand on the Oral Law, Karaite creed does not differ in its essentials from that of Rabbanite Judaism. Unlike Rabbanite Judaism, Karaism has no fixed number of commandments (of commission or omission). Karaite legal doctrine does not, of course, even approach rabbinic Judaism in its multi-faceted development. In particular, Karaism lacks systematic development and interpretation of biblical law. The calendar, laws of marriage, and precepts on ritual purity have received the most intensive treatment in Karaism, usually in a strictly literal sense and with a tendency toward greater severity.

Special rules apply to the sanctification of the Sabbath. Prohibition of work extends, beyond the 39 actions proscribed by Rabbanite Judaism, to any action not forming part of the prayer service or not absolutely necessary for nourishment or the satisfaction of other physical human needs. The earlier Karaite teachers prohibited the kindling of lights on Friday for use on the Sabbath and even taught that a light already lit had to be extinguished on the Sabbath. To this day, however, Karaites are either "friends of light" or "enemies of light," depending on whether or not they use artificial light on the Sabbath. Sexual intercourse is also prohibited on the Sabbath, and Karaites also oppose a number of alleviations of Sabbath precepts sanctioned by the rabbis.

Certain rabbinical precepts pertaining to circumcision (*peri'ah* and *meẓiẓah*) are rejected by the Karaites. They also differ on the detailed regulations of ritual slaughter, and therefore regard the meat of animals slaughtered according to Rabbanite regulations as prohibited.

Karaite laws on marriage and the prohibited degrees of consanguinity are of special severity. In the early period, even the farthest removed degree of consanguinity was regarded as prohibited, with the result that by the 11th century the Karaite community was running the danger of extinction. This extreme theory of incest was rejected and replaced by a less stringent law consisting of a set of six regulations.

Karaite liturgy—which originally consisted solely of biblical psalmody—has the least similarity with its Rabbanite counterpart. There are two prayer services a day, mornings and evenings; on the Sabbath and holy days the additional prayer and other nonobligatory prayers are added. Originally, the *Ma'amadot* (prayers referring to the Temple sacrifices) formed the main basis of the Karaite rite. A prayer may be short or long, but must consist of seven parts, and the confession of faith. The prayers consist mainly of passages from the Bible (with the emphasis on Psalms) and partly also of prayer-poems, unknown to the Rabbanite rite. The *Shema* prayer is included in the Karaite rite, but the *Shemoneh-Esreh* (daily prayer consisting of 18 benedictions) is not known. The *haftarot* selection used by the Karaites   79 differs from the Rabbanite one. During the prayer service, Karaites wear *ẓiẓit* (a fringed garment), the *ẓiẓit* including a light-blue thread. The biblical prescriptions concerning *mezuzah* and *tefillin* are regarded by the Karaites as having a figurative and symbolic meaning and they reject the rabbinical regulations based on them.

6 DRUZE

The Druze, their name derived from al-Darazī, one of the founders of the sect, is a religio-political community inhabiting parts of Syria, Lebanon, and Israel. The Druze are set apart from other groups primarily by their adherence to a separate religion. Their language is Arabic and in overall cultural and social patterns they are not appreciably different from the villagers and mountaineers among whom they live. The factors keeping them apart include the effective prohibition against intermarriage with other communities, the non-admission of converts, a number of individual customs, a long history of armed conflict against intolerant rulers and rival groups, and a strong sense of communal separateness and group solidarity. In the 1960s their total number was estimated at approximately 300,000: approximately 155,000 in Syria (the great majority in the Jebel el-Druz Province), approximately 110,000 in Lebanon (mostly in the provinces of Mt. Lebanon and al-Biqāʿ), and 33,000 in Israel (in 18 villages, mostly in Upper Galilee, some also in Lower Galilee and Mt. Carmel). In June 1967 several Druze villages of the Golan (province of Quneitra), totaling about 6,000 inhabitants, came under Israel rule.

HISTORY. The Druze religion has its roots in Ismailism, a religio-political movement which, after years of underground activity, founded the Fatimid Caliphate in the tenth century. The Druze community originated in the reign of al-Ḥākim bi-Amr-Allah (996–1021), the sixth Caliph of the Ismaʿili Fatimid dynasty. Active proselytizing to the new

Prime Minister David Ben-Gurion at Julis with Druze leaders, Sheikh Amin Tarif (center), and two members of the Knesset, Sheikh Jabar Mouadi (left) and Sheikh Saleh Khnefis (right), July 1959. Courtesy Government Press Office, Tel Aviv.

creed was brief and had lasting results only in some of the remoter parts of the caliph's domains. Since about 1050 the community has been closed to outsiders. It has not moved far from the regions where the original conversions were made.

The first testimony on the Druze in non-Arab literature occurs in the book of travels by Benjamin of Tudela, who toured Syria about 1167. Little is known of the history of the Druze until the Ottoman conquest of Syria (1516). On that occasion, the Emir Fakhr al-Dīn, of the house of Maʿan, helped the sultan Selim I, who confirmed him as Emir of the Druze. They lived in southern Lebanon and northern Palestine, in many of the villages where they are still found, and were a separate, "unbelieving," and warlike community. Their sheikhs and emirs had evidently succeeded in gaining a certian amount of local autonomy, especially on Mt. Lebanon, for, from the Ottoman conquest of Syria and Palestine, there gradually emerged a sort of semi-autonomous emirate that was based, in large measure, on Druze military power and feudal organization. This emirate was centered in Mt. Lebanon. Until the 18th century relations between Lebanese Druze and their neighbors, especially the Maronite Christians, were tolerably good, but they later deteriorated. Civil strife between Druze and Maronites lasted until 1860, when the bloody events of that year ended in an intervention by the great powers and, eventually, in the special autonomous administration of Mt. Lebanon within the Ottoman Empire. The net result of the complex political settlement was a defeat for the Druze, who have never since regained their ascendancy in the Lebanon region.

The main center of the community after 1869 passed to Mt. Hauran, where a Druze settlement had been established approximately one hundred years earlier by immigrants from Lebanon; Mt. Hauran then became known as Jebel el-Druze ("Mountain of the Druze"), a name that had formerly been synonymous with Mt. Lebanon. There the Druze were governed, largely by the emirs of the al-Aṭrash house, as a semi-autonomous community until the end of Ottoman rule in 1918. In 1921 the French tried to set up an autonomous Druze state under French mandate, but this failed and, in 1925, the Druze rose against the French, spearheading a general Syrian uprising.

In Galilee there probably were Druze settlements as early as the 11th or 12th century, and the presence of such settlements is clearly documented from the 13th century on. The Galilean Druze seem always to have kept close contact with the other branches of the community, especially those of Mt. Hermon and southern Lebanon, but do not seem to have participated as a group in the events which called the attention of the world to their brethren. During the British

Faris Feillah, the first Druze judge in Israel, being sworn in by President Shazar, October 1968. Courtesy Government Press Office, Tel Aviv.

Mandate over Palestine they refrained, by and large, from taking part in the Arab-Israel conflict, and, during the 1948 War of Independence, turned this watchful neutrality into active participation in fighting on the Jewish side. Druze have since then served in the Israel Defence Forces, at first as volunteers and later within the framework of the regular draft system. Many Druze also serve in the Israel Border Police. They thus opted squarely against the mainstream of Arab nationalism and for integration in Israel.

Since 1957 the Druze have been given official recognition in Israel as a separate religious community. In 1962 the Knesset set up official Druze communal courts, which had previously functioned without official sanction. The spiritual leadership of the community is in the hands of its sheikhs from the various centers of Druze population.

RELIGION. The Druze religion, which Druze call *Dīn al-Tawḥīd* ("unitarianism" or "monotheism"), is based on principies derived essentially from Ismailism (Ismāʿīliyya), some of which originate in Neoplatonism and are common to a number of gnostic sects. It includes a belief in a deity that operates in the world through a system of five cosmic principles, or "emanations"; a belief in periodic human manifestations of the deity and the emanations; and esoteric interpretations of the "revealed" religions whose recognized prophets (e.g., Moses, Jesus, Muhammad) were the bearers of esoteric truths only. The inner meaning of these prophets' mission, in each case, is secretly propagated to a select group by an incarnation of the first cosmic principle, or "Universal Mind." During the time of Moses, that incarnation was Shuʿayb, or Jethro, Moses' father-in-law; Druze pay homage to his putative grave near Hittim in Galilee. The Druze have few ceremonials or rituals, and initiate only a very few members of the community into the precepts of the religion, which are not published or discussed in the outside world at all. Though their religion has its roots in a form of Islam, they are not Muslims.

A celebration at Nabī Shuʿayb, eastern Galilee, venerated by the Druzes as the grave of Jethro, father-in-law of Moses. Courtesy Keren Hayesod United Jewish Appeal, Jerusalem.

7 THE BAHĀ'Ī

The Bahā'ī faith is a world religion which established its center in Ereẓ Israel. Named after its founder, Bahā' Allāh ("The Splendor of God"), Bahaism developed out of the Bābī, a Ṣufi (Muslim mystical) movement, which was founded in 1844 in Persia. It upholds the unity of God, enjoins its followers to search after truth, and advocates promotion of unity and concord among peoples. It maintains equality of rights for men and women, prohibits monasticism, advocates an auxiliary international language, and has abolished priesthood. The faith inculcates the principle of the oneness and wholeness of the entire human race.

Sayyid Ali Muhammad, the founder of the Bābī movement, was born in Shiraz, Persia, between 1818 and 1821 and was brought up as a member of a Shī'-Ṣufi sect. Some Shī'ītes and the Ṣufis believe that in each age there is a man, called the Bāb ("Gate"), who initiates in the secrets of the faith. To the Bābīs he is the "Gate" to the knowledge of divine truth. In 1844 Ali Muhammad proclaimed himself the Bāb of his time and was accused of heresy. He was arrested and shot in Tabriz in 1850. His body was interred by his followers in a secret tomb in Teheran.

In 1852 an attempt on the life of the Persian shah, Nāṣir al-Dīn, was followed by severe persecution of the Bābīs, which led the Bāb's successor, Mirzā (Persian, "prince") Yaḥyā, and the latter's stepbrother, Mirzā Ḥusayn Ali (b. 1817), to flee to Baghdad. In 1863 the Turkish government, at Persia's request, exiled Mirzā Yaḥyā to Cyprus.

Mirzā Ḥusayn Ali proclaimed himself the successor to the Bāb under the name Bahā' Allāh. The government exiled him to Adrianople (1864) and later to Acre, which he reached in 1868, accompanied by about 70 of his family and followers. It was he who turned the faith into a universalist ethical religion, of which he became the leader. In 1899 he had the body of Ali Muhammad, the Bāb, transferred from its tomb in Teheran to Acre. The Bahā' Allāh died in 1892, and his tomb in the village of Mazra'a (near Acre) in a building at Bahjī (Persian, "garden") became a shrine that the Bahā'īs regard as the holiest place in the world.

Bahā' Allāh's eldest son, 'Abbās Effendi, became the leader of the faith under the name of 'Abd al-Bahā' ("the Servant of Bahā'"). After transferring his residence to Haifa, he set out on travels to North Africa, Europe, and the U.S. 'Abbās Effendi arranged for the interment of the Bāb's body in a shrine in Haifa on Mount Carmel.

The golden-domed Bahai Temple on Mount Carmel, Haifa, completed in 1953. Courtesy Government Press Office, Tel Aviv.

'Abd al-Bahā' ('Abbās Effendi) died in 1921 and was interred in the same shrine.

The great mausoleum (Maqām-i A'la), which is a landmark in Haifa, was only completed in 1953. 'Abd al-Bahā' was succeeded by his eldest grandson, Shoghi Effendi Rabbānī (1897–1957), who as guardian of the Bahā'ī faith resided in Haifa.

The faith spread all over the world; Bahā'īs reside in over 11,000 localities. The spiritual and administrative center of the Bahā'ī World Faith is the Universal House of Justice (erected in 1963 in Haifa), comprising, in the Holy Land nine members, known as Hands of the Cause.

Bahaism was favorably disposed to Zionism, believing that the return of the Jews to their land was foretold in the writings of Bahā' Allāh and 'Abad al-Bahā'. On June 30, 1948, Shoghi Effendi wrote to Prime Minister Ben-Gurion expressing "loyalty and best wishes for the prosperity of the newly proclaimed State of Israel" and recognizing the significance of the ingathering of the Jews in "the cradle of their faith."

Part Two:

RELIGIOUS LEGAL AND JUDICIAL SYSTEM

1 JUDICIARY AND LEGISLATION

Judiciary. Throughout the period from the promulgation of the Ottoman Constitution of 1876 until the present time there have been both secular and religious courts exercising jurisdiction in the territory of the land of Israel, but the extent of the jurisdiction of such courts, the qualifications of the judges thereof and of the persons authorized to plead therein, the procedure thereof and the language of pleading therein have varied from time to time.

UNDER THE OTTOMAN EMPIRE (1876–1917). The Ottoman Constitution of 1876 provided that cases under Shariʿa (Muslim religious) law had to be heard by the Shariʿa Courts. These Courts were given jurisdiction in matters not within the jurisdiction of the Civil Courts, such as property in waqf (Muslim religious trust), inhibitions and the termination of inhibitions, wills, the appointment and removal of guardians and trustees, and the granting of loans from the estates of orphans and waqf estates. They also had jurisdiction to hear suits to decide the shares of heirs to property and suits relating to estates in which letters of administration had to be taken out, as well as all other suits concerning rights under the Shariʿa law. Where the parties before a Shariʿa Court made a written agreement that a matter in dispute should be dealt with by the Shariʿa Court, although it was within the jurisdiction of the Civil Court, no application could subsequently be entertained in the matter by the Civil Court. The Ministry of Justice in Constantinople exercised administrative powers in regard to the procedure and internal organization of the Shariʿa

Courts, the rules of procedure for which were established by law. The Jewish and Christian Religious Courts had jurisdiction over members of their respective communities in matters of personal status.

BRITISH MILITARY ADMINISTRATION, 1917–1920. One of the first acts of the British Military Administration in the Occupied Enemy Territory of Palestine was to reestablish the courts, reopening them in Jerusalem on July 24, 1918. The head of the legal department of the British Military Administration, appointed the judges of the Muslim Religious Courts after consultation with a committee composed of the Muslim members of the Court of Appeal and the inspectors of the Shari'a Courts.

BRITISH CIVIL ADMINISTRATION, 1920–48. *Religious Courts.* In regard to matters of personal status, namely, suits regarding marriage or divorce, alimony, maintenance, guardianship, legitimation and adoption of minors, inhibition from dealing with property of persons who are legally incompetent, successions, wills and legacies, and the administration of the property of absent persons, jurisdiction was conferred by the Palestine Order-in-Council, 1922, upon the courts of the religious communities established and exercising jurisdiction at the date of the Order (Sept. 1, 1922), namely the Muslim Religious Courts, the Rabbinical Courts, and the courts of the nine recognized Christian communities: Eastern (Orthodox), Latin (Catholic), Gregorian Armenian, Armenian (Catholic), Syrian (Catholic), Chaldean (Uniate), Greek (Catholic) Malkite, Maronite, and Syrian Orthodox. The Muslim Religious Courts were given exclusive jurisdiction in matters of personal status of Muslims and also exclusive jurisdiction in cases of the constitution or internal administration of a waqf constituted for the benefit of Muslims before a Muslim Religious Court, and there was an appeal from the court of the qadi to the Muslim Religious Court of Appeal, whose decision was final. The Rabbinical Courts of the Jewish community and the courts of the several Christian communities had exclusive jurisdiction in matters of marriage and divorce, alimony and confirmation of wills of members of their community, other than foreigners, and jurisdiction in any other matter of personal status of such persons, where all the parties to the action consented to their jurisdiction. The Rabbinical Courts and the courts of the several Christian communities, also had exclusive jurisdiction over any case as to the constitution or internal administration of a waqf or religious endowment constituted before these courts according to the religious law of the community concerned.

Matters of personal status affecting foreigners other than Muslims were within the jurisdiction of the District Courts, but those courts had no jurisdiction to pronounce a decree of dissolution of marriage. Foreigners could consent to matters of personal status being tried by the courts of the religious communities having jurisdiction in like matters affecting Palestinian citizens, but such courts, other than Muslim Religious Courts, had no power to grant a decree of dissolution of marriage to a foreign subject. Where any action of personal status involved persons of different religious communities, application could be made by any party to the chief justice, who was required, with the assistance, if he thought fit, of assessors from the communities concerned, to decide which court should have jurisdiction. Whenever a question arose as to whether or not a case was one of personal status within the exclusive jurisdiction of a Religious Court, the matter had to be referred to a Special Tribunal composed of two British judges of the Supreme Court and the president of the highest court in Palestine of the religious community concerned, or a judge appointed by him. The chief justice or the senior puisne judge of the Supreme Court, presided over the Tribunal.

The jurisdiction of the Rabbinical Courts and the Christian Religious Courts remained unchanged throughout the period of the Mandatory regime, but that of the Muslim Religious Courts was altered by the Palestine Amendment Order-in-Council, 1939, whereunder they could exercise jurisdiction over Muslims who were foreign-

ers only if, according to their national law, Muslim

Religious Courts had jurisdiction over them in matters of personal status. No provision was made in the Palestine Order-in-Council, 1922, for the granting by the courts of orders or decrees in connection with the marriage of persons neither of whom was a Muslim or a member of the Jewish community or of any of the nine recognized Christian communities, or for the dissolution or annulment of such marriages. The Palestine Amendment Order-in-Council, 1939, authorized the making by ordinance of provision for such matters, but no such ordinance was enacted.

Appointment and Qualifications of Judges. The qadis of the Muslim Religious Courts, the president and the various members of the Muslim Religious Court of Appeal and the inspectors of the Muslim Religious Courts were nominated by the Supreme Muslim Shari'a Council for approval by the Palestine Government and, after such approval, were appointed by that council, the president and members whereof received salaries from the Palestine government in consideration of their services in connection with the affairs of the Muslim Religious Courts. Under the Jewish Community Rules each Rabbinical Office sat as a Rabbinical Court of First Instance, and the Rabbinical Council was the Court of Appeal in matters in which the Rabbinical Courts had jurisdiction. The judges of the courts of the recognized Christian religious communities were appointed by the heads of the communities.

Qualifications of Advocates. Applicants wishing to obtain a license to practice before the Muslim Religious Courts had to satisfy the Legal Board that they were adequately qualified by examination as to their knowledge of Muslim law and were of good character, or that they were so certified by the Supreme Muslim Shari'a Council. Advocates alleged to be guilty of disgraceful, fraudulent, or unprofessional conduct were subject to Courts of Discipline constituted by, and subject to the control of the chief justice. Until the ordinance was amended in 1930, no woman could be granted a license to practice as an **93** advocate. That disqualification was removed by the amending ordinance, but a woman holding such a license did not have the right of audience in a Tribal Court or in a Muslim Religious Court unless she was certified by the Supreme Muslim Shariʿa Council to be qualified to practice. Under the Law Council Ordinance, 1938, the Legal Board was replaced by the Law Council, which was composed of not less than six members appointed by the high commissioner of whom not less than four had to be practicing advocates, with the attorney general as ex officio chairman. It was also empowered to inquire into the conduct of advocates and persons permitted to practice before the Muslim Religious Courts.

IN THE STATE OF ISRAEL—FROM 1948. Under section 17 of the Law and Administration Ordinance, 1948, of the Provisional Council of State, the courts existing in the territory of the State of Israel were empowered to continue to function within the scope of the powers conferred upon them by law so long as no new law concerning the courts was enacted.

Religious Courts. Changes in the jurisdiction of the Religious Courts were made by the Israel Legislature, particularly as regards the rabbinical courts, as the Jewish Community Rules were inapplicable in the State of Israel.

Under the Rabbinical Courts Jurisdiction (Marriage and Divorce) Law, 1953, the rabbinical courts have exclusive jurisdiction in matters of marriage and divorce of Jews in Israel, who are nationals or residents of the state, in any matter connected with a suit for divorce between Jews which has been filed therein, whether by the wife or the husband, including maintenance for the wife and for the children of the couple, and claims for *ḥaliẓah* filed therein by a woman against her deceased husband's brother, including maintenance for the woman until the day when *ḥaliẓah* is given. Furthermore, when a Jewish wife sues her Jewish husband or his estate for maintenance in a rabbinical court, otherwise than in connection with divorce, 94 the plea of the defendant that a rabbinical court has no

The Supreme Rabbinical Court in session at Hechal Shlomo, Jerusalem. Left to right: Jacob Adess, Ovadia Hadya, and Bezalel Zolti. Courtesy Government Press Office, Tel Aviv.

jurisdiction in the matter may not be entertained, and in matters of personal status of Jews in which a rabbinical court has not exclusive jurisdiction under the law, it will have jurisdiction after all the parties concerned have expressed their consent thereto. Upon the coming into force of the Adoption of Children Law, 1960, the adoption of children was excluded from the definition of matters of **95** personal status in the Palestine Order-in-Council; so were successions, wills and legacies upon the coming into force of the Inheritance Law 1965. Jurisdiction in matters of adoption under the above law is conferred upon Religious Courts, however, if the parents, the adopters, and the adoptee have consented in writing to their jurisdiction, or, in the case of an adoptee not being capable of understanding the matter, or being under the age of 13 years, if a social welfare officer and the attorney general have consented to their jurisdiction. Under the Inheritance Law, 1965, a Religious Court which had jurisdiction in matters of personal status of the decedent may make an order of inheritance or an order confirming a will and determine rights to maintenance from the estate if all the parties concerned according to the law have expressed in writing their consent thereto.

The Druze Religious Courts Law, 1962, established, for the first time in Israel, a Druze Religious Court and a Druze Religious Court of Appeal. The Druze Religious Court is given exclusive jurisdiction in matters of marriage and divorce of Druze in Israel who are nationals or residents of the state and matters relating to the creation or internal management of a religious trust established before a court under Druze religious law or of a Druze trust established before the coming into force of the Law in accordance with Druze custom otherwise than before a religious or civil court. In matters of personal status of Druze in which a Druze Religious Court has no exclusive jurisdiction under the law, such court will have jurisdiction after all the parties concerned have expressed their consent. The Druze Religious Court of Appeal has jurisdiction to deal with appeals from judgments of the Druze Religious Courts.

Matters of dissolution of marriage, including divorce, annulment of marriage, and recognition of a marriage as void *ab initio,* which are not within the exclusive jurisdiction of a Jewish, Muslim, Christian, or Druze Religious Court, are within the jurisdiction of the District Court or a

Religious Court as determined by the president of the

Supreme Court in accordance with the provisions of the Jurisdiction in Matters of Dissolution of Marriage (Special Cases) Law, 1969. That law will not apply if both spouses are Jews, Muslims, Druze or members of one of the Christian communities maintaining a Religious Court in Israel. In cases to which the law applies, the provisions of the Palestine Order in Council prohibiting the District Courts and Religious Courts from granting decrees of dissolution of marriage will not apply. When a District Court upon which jurisdiction has been conferred under the law deals with the matter it must do so in accordance with the following order of priority: (1) the internal law of the place of permanent residence common to the spouses; (2) the internal law of the last place of permanent residence common to the spouses; (3) the internal law of the country of the common nationality of the spouses; (4) the internal law of the place where the marriage was celebrated; but it may not deal with the matter according to a law as aforesaid if according thereto different laws are applicable to both the spouses. If there is no law applicable as aforesaid, the court may deal with the matter in accordance with the internal law of the place of permanent residence of one of the spouses as appears to it just in the circumstances of the case, but the consent of the spouses will always be a ground for divorce.

The Supreme Court has jurisdiction to order Religious Courts to deal with a particular matter in accordance with their competence or to refrain from dealing or from continuing to deal with a particular matter otherwise than in accordance with their competence, but it may not entertain a petition in relation thereto unless the petitioner has raised the question of competence at the earliest opportunity; where he has not had a reasonable opportunity to raise the question of competence before the decision was given by the Religious Court, the Supreme Court may quash a proceeding taken, or decision given, by the Religious Court without authority.

Appointment and Qualifications of Judges, etc. Under the

Judges Law, 1953, an entirely new system of appointment was created: all the judges of the Magistrates' Courts, the District Courts and the Supreme Court are appointed by the president of the state upon the recommendation of a Nominations Committee submitted to him by the minister of justice, who is its chairman.

Similar systems of appointment have been created for judges of the Rabbinical Courts, the Muslim Religious Courts, and the Druze Religious Courts, but no legislation has yet been passed regulating the appointment of the judges of the Christian Religious Courts, who continue to be appointed by the head of the community. Under the Dayyanim Law, 5715—1955, the judges of the Rabbinical Courts, known as *dayyanim* are appointed by the president of the state upon the recommendation of a Nominations Committee submitted to him by the minister for religious affairs. The committee is composed of the two chief rabbis of Israel, two *dayyanim* elected by the body of *dayyanim* for three years, two members of the government, namely, the minister for religious affairs and one other member chosen by the government, two members of the Knesset elected by it by secret ballot, and two practicing advocates elected by the Chamber of Advocates. Persons qualified in accordance with regulations made by the minister for religious affairs with the consent of the Chief Rabbinate Council are eligible for appointment as *dayyanim* if they were so qualified within the two years preceding the appointment. Under those regulations they must have a rabbinical certificate authorizing them to teach and adjudicate issued by an expert rabbi or torah institute whose certificate is recognized by the Chief Rabbinate Council, be 30 years of age, be or have been married, and have a character and mode of life which befit the status of a *dayyan* in Israel. In addition, a *dayyan* of a Rabbinical Court must have passed examinations held on behalf of the Chief Rabbinate Council or be exempted therefrom, while a *dayyan* of the Rabbinical Court of Appeal must have been a *dayyan* of a Rabbinical Court for at least three consecutive years, or be known as an illustrious Torah scholar *(gadol ba-Torah)* according to a majority of the members of the Council of the Chief Rabbinate Council including the two chief rabbis. The subjects of the examination for *dayyanim* are: (1) general knowledge of the Talmud and the *Posekim;* (2) thorough knowledge of the Shulḥan Arukh, *Even ha-Ezer* and *Ḥoshen Mishpat;* (3) drafting of a judgment in a hypothetical case with reasoned findings of fact and decisions of substantive law; (4) knowledge of the rules and procedure based upon the *halakhah.*

Under the Qadis Law, 1961, the judges of the Muslim Religious Courts, known as qadis, are appointed by the president of the state upon the recommendation of a Nominations Committee submitted to him by the minister for religious affairs. The Nominations Committee is composed of two qadis elected by the body of qadis for three years, two members of the government, namely, the minister for religious affairs and one other member chosen by the government, three members of the Knesset, including at least two Muslims, elected by the Knesset by secret ballot, and two advocates, including at least one Muslim, appointed by the Chamber of Advocates. Persons qualified to be appointed as qadis are Muslims who have had suitable training in Shari'a Law, whose way of life and character befit the status of a qadi in the State of Israel and who are at least 30 years of age and are, or have been, married.

Under the Druze Religious Courts Law, 1962, judges of the Druze Religious Courts, known as qadis *madhhab,* are appointed by the president of the state upon the recom- mendation of a Nominations Committee submitted to him by the minister for religious affairs. The Nominations Committee is composed of the chairman of the Druze Religious Council constituted by rules made by the minister for religious affairs under the Religious Communities (Organization) Ordinance, the president of the Druze Religious Court of Appeal, or, if he serves also as the chairman of the Druze Religious Council, a qadi *madhhab* elected by the body of qadis *madhhab* for three years, another qadi *madhhab* similarly elected, the minister for religious affairs and the minister of justice, two Druze members of the Knesset (or other Druze, if there is only one Druze member of the Knesset or none) elected by the Knesset by secret ballot and an advocate elected by the National Council of the Chamber of Advocates for three years. Persons qualified to be appointed as qadis *madhhab* are Druze who have had a suitable training in Druze religious law, whose way of life and character befit the status of a qadi *madhhab* in the State of Israel and who are at least 30 years of age and are, or have been, married. As from July 9, 1964, no person may be appointed as a judge, *dayyan,* qadi, or qadi *madhhab* of the courts to which the above laws apply, unless he is an Israel citizen. If the candidate for appointment has also another nationality and the laws of the state in which he is a national enable him to divest himself of such nationality, he will not be appointed until after he has done everything necessary on his part in order to divest himself thereof.

Every person appointed as a judge, *dayyan,* qadi, or qadi *madhhab* must, before assuming his office, make before the president of the state a declaration whereby he pledges himself to bear allegiance to the State of Israel, to dispense justice fairly, not to pervert the law and to show no favor, while every judge must also pledge himself to bear allegiance to the laws of the State of Israel. Every judge, qadi, and qadi *madhhab* in judicial matters is expressly declared by the law applicable to him to be subject to no authority other than that of the law, while under the Dayyanim Law, 1955, every *dayyan* in judicial matters is expressly to be subject to no authority other than that of the law according to which he judges. The reason for the difference in wording as regards the *dayyanim* is to make it clear that only the laws concerning the legal system of the *dayyanim,* including those laws which restrict the jurisdiction of the *dayyanim* and no other laws, bind the *dayyanim* in judicial matters. Every judge, *dayyan,* qadi, and qadi *madhhab* will hold office from the day of his declaration of allegiance and his tenure will end only upon his death, resignation, retirement on pension, or removal from office by virtue of the law applicable to him. He may resign his office by submitting a letter of resignation to the appropriate minister, and his tenure of office will terminate upon the expiration of three months from the submission of the letter of resignation, unless the minister has consented to a shorter period. He may retire on pension if he has attained the age of 60 having held office for 20 years, or if he has attained the age of 65 after having held office for 15 years and if he so requests and his request is approved by the appropriate Nominations Committee. He must retire if the appropriate Nominations Committee, on the strength of a medical opinion, decides that, owing to his state of health, he is unable to continue in office, or on attaining the age of 70 years, unless he is a chief rabbi of Israel or a senior presiding *dayyan,* in which case he must retire on pension on attaining the age of 75 years.

Every judge, *dayyan,* qadi and qadi *madhhab* is subject to the jurisdiction of a Court of Discipline constituted under the law applicable to him. The Court of Discipline for judges consists of five members, including three judges of the Supreme Court, as the president of the Supreme Court may in respect of each case prescribe, and its members are appointed in respect of each case by the body of the judges of the Supreme Court. Similar provisions apply, *mutatis mutandis,* to *dayyanim.* The courts of discipline for qadis and qadis *madhhab* consist of three members: the president of the Shariʿa Court of Appeal or the Druze Religious Court of Appeal, as the case may be, or the qadi or qadi *madhhab,* as the case may be with the greatest length of service, an advocate appointed for each case by the National Council of the Chamber of Advocates, and one member appointed for each case by the minister of religious affairs. The minister of justice may submit a complaint against a judge, and the minister for religious affairs against a *dayyan,* a qadi or a qadi *madhhab,* to the competent Court of Discipline on one of the following grounds: (1) he has acted improperly in carrying out his functions; (2) he has behaved in a manner unbecoming his judicial status in the State of Israel; (3) he has been convicted of an offense which in the circumstances of the case involves moral turpitude; (4) the Nominations Committee has found that he obtained his appointment unlawfully. The Court of Discipline must submit its findings, whether favorable or unfavorable, to the appropriate minister; if it finds that the person concerned is unworthy to continue in his functions, the minister must submit its findings to the president of the state, who must remove him from office. Criminal proceedings may not be brought against a judge, *dayyan,* qadi or qadi *madhhab* save by the attorney general before a District Court composed of three judges. The salaries and other payments to be made to a judge, *dayyan,* qadi and qadi *madhhab* during and after his period of tenure, including those to be made to his dependents after his death, are fixed by resolution of the Knesset or by the Finance Committee of the Knesset if so authorized by the Knesset.

Legislation. UNDER THE OTTOMAN EMPIRE. Under the Ottoman Constitution of 1876 the sultan was empowered to sanction and promulgate all legislation, to make proposals for all kinds of laws, and to safeguard and enforce the rules of the Shariʿa and the laws of the state. Islam was the religion of the Ottoman Empire, but subject thereto the state was required to protect the free exercise of all religions recognized in the empire and the integral enjoyment, in accordance with previous practice, of all religious privileges granted to the various communities, provided that such religions were not contrary to public morals or conducive to the disturbance of public order. All Ottoman subjects were equal in the eyes of the law as regards both rights and duties, except for matters relating to religion. Turkish was the official language of the state.

The Ottoman laws were of three categories: those written originally in Turkish, those written originally in Arabic and translated into Turkish, and those written originally in a

European language, mainly French, and translated into Turkish. The most important of those laws written originally in Arabic is the Mejelle, an elaborate code of 1,851 articles containing rules of law and maxims of Muhammadan jurisprudence. It is little more than a Turkish translation from the Arab authorities on Muhammadan law, which is based primarily on the Koran and custom. The substantive part of the Mejelle is arranged in 16 books dealing with: sale, hire, guarantee, transfer of debt, pledges, trusts and trusteeship, gift, wrongful appropriation and destruction, interdiction, constraint and preemption, joint ownership, agency, settlement and release, admissions, actions, evidence and administration of oath, and administration of justice by the court.

UNDER THE MANDATE. Under the Mandate for Palestine, confirmed by the Council of the League of Nations on July 24, 1922, His Britannic Majesty, who had been selected by the principal Allied Powers as mandatory for Palestine, was given full powers of legislation and of administration in Palestine save as such powers were limited by the terms of the Mandate. Under article 15, the mandatory was required to ensure complete freedom of conscience and the free exercise of all forms of worship for all, subject only to the maintenance of public order and morals. There was to be no discrimination of any kind between the inhabitants of Palestine on grounds of race, religion, or language, and no one was to be excluded from the country on the sole ground of his religious belief.

The Palestine Order-in-Council, 1922, was made by His Britannic Majesty by virtue and in exercise of his powers in that behalf by the U. K. Foreign Jurisdiction Act, 1890 or otherwise, and came into force on Sept. 1, 1922. It provided (article 46) that the jurisdiction of the civil courts should be exercised in conformity with the Ottoman law in force in Palestine on Nov. 1, 1914 (the date when Turkey entered World War I), such later Ottoman laws as had been or might be declared to be in force by public notice, and such orders-in-council, ordinances, and regulations as were in **103** force in Palestine at the date of the commencement of the order (Sept. 1, 1922) or might thereafter be applied or enacted.

However, no ordinance could be promulgated which restricted complete freedom of conscience and the free exercise of all forms of worship, save insofar as was required for the maintenance of public order and morals, or which tended to discriminate in any way between the inhabitants of Palestine on the ground of race, religion, or language; or which was in any way repugnant to, or inconsistent with, the provisions of the Mandate.

For the most part, by the time the Mandate was terminated, Palestine legislation had replaced the Ottoman law which formed part of the law of Palestine on Nov. 1, 1914, when Turkey entered the war, although some important parts of it, including part of the civil law (Mejelle) and the Land Law, were not replaced. Thus, for example, the commercial and criminal law and the law of civil and criminal procedure were replaced by Palestine legislation modeled upon English law adapted to local circumstances.

IN THE STATE OF ISRAEL. On May 14, 1948, the Declaration of Independence proclaiming the establishment of the State of Israel was issued by the National Council (Mo'eẓet ha-Am), which consisted of 37 representatives of the *yishuv* and the Zionist movement. The council declared that the various laws which existed in Palestine on May 14, 1948, should be in force in Israel insofar as would be consistent with the provisions of the proclamation, with any future laws passed by or with the authority of the Provisional Council of State, and with the modifications emanating from the establishment of the state and its authorities.

The first law to be enacted by the Provisional Council of State was the Law and Administration Ordinance, 1948, passed on May 19, with retroactive effect from May 14, 1948. It provided that the Provisional Council of State was the legislative authority and its executive arm, the National

Administration (Minhelet ha-Am) was the provisional government.

During the nine months of its existence (May 14, 1948–Feb. 14, 1949), the Provisional Council of State enacted 98 ordinances and the various ministers made 34 sets of emergency regulations. On November 18, 1948, ten days after a census of the population was taken, the Provisional Council of State passed an ordinance providing for the holding of elections to the Constituent Assembly of 120 members. On Feb. 14, 1949, the Constituent Assembly held its inaugural meeting, and two days later it passed its first law, the Transition Law, 1949, which provided that the legislature of Israel was to be known as the "Knesset," and the Constituent Assembly as the "First Knesset," and that the legislative acts of the Israel legislature should henceforth be known as "laws."

The vast majority of the laws passed by the Israel legislature have their counterparts in the legislation of most other countries, but some of them are peculiar to Israel, owing to its being a Jewish state and the realization of the aims of Zionism. Among these are the Law of Return, passed by the Knesset on July 5, 1950, under which the right of every Jew to settle in Israel is recognized. Laws relating to Jewish law and religion cover such subjects as *kasher* food for soldiers (1948), Jewish religious services budgets (1949), the Chief Rabbinate Council (1955), the jurisdiction of religious courts in marriage and divorce (1953), *dayyanim* (1955), and the prohibition of pig breeding (1962). Furthermore, whenever legislation is required on any particular subject, the relevant principles of Jewish law, if any, are examined and, if found suitable, incorporated. Original Israel laws relating to non-Jewish communities deal with qadis (Muslim religious judges) and the composition and authority of Druze religious courts. On June 27, 1967, less than two weeks after the Six-Day War, the Knesset passed a law for the protection of all holy places under Israel jurisdiction. Nearly all that was left of the Mejelle has been replaced by Israel legislation.

2 JEWISH LAW

The Official Position Assigned to Jewish Law. On the establishment of the State of Israel, Jewish law continued to occupy the same official position in the legal structure of the state as it had done in the pre-state period. The Law and Administration Ordinance of 1948 prescribed that the law in existence on the eve of establishment of the state should remain in force (sec. 11), with the practical result that officially Jewish law was incorporated in the area of personal status only. At the same time the Hebrew language celebrated its final victory, even in a formal sense, and section 15b of the above ordinance repealed any provision in any law requiring the use of English, thus making Hebrew the language of the state, of its law, and of its everyday life.

MATTERS OF PERSONAL STATUS. The jurisdiction of the rabbinical courts was defined in a Knesset law of 1953 which, save for one or two changes, entailed no substantial departure from the existing situation. It gave the rabbinical courts exclusive jurisdiction in matters of marriage, divorce, and *ḥaliẓah;* as regards the wife's claim for maintenance, jurisdiction is given to the court to which the wife applies—the rabbinical or the district court. In this and in other laws there were also prescribed the circumstances in which the rabbinical courts have concurrent jurisdiction in other matters of personal status.

THE RABBINICAL COURTS. Matters entrusted to the jurisdiction of the rabbinical courts are naturally dealt with in accordance with Jewish law. In the course of their activities these courts have given decisions introducing a number of important innovations in Jewish law, such as a married woman's right to the income deriving from the pursuit of her own profession, and recognition of the existence of mutual pecuniary rights between spouses married abroad in a civil ceremony only, and so on (see M. Elon, *Ḥakikah Datit . . .,* 166–72). In certain matters the law prescribes that the rabbinical courts too must decide in accordance with the general law. In the Succession Ordinance of 1923 provision was made for the treatment of son and daughter, husband and wife, on terms of equality as regards the division of certain kinds of property on succession, and the Women's Equal Rights Law, 1951, extended the directive to all other property. Some of the other main provisions of this law are the following: men and women are equated as regards all legal acts; the father and mother are given natural guardianship of their children; a married woman is given full capacity of acquisition during marriage and retention of her rights to property acquired by her prior to the marriage. In addition this law allows the litigants, if they are above the age of 18 years, to consent to having their case tried according to the laws of their community. It also states that its provisions shall not affect any halakhic prohibition or permission relating to marriage or divorce. In the main its provisions accord with the position under Jewish law as it has evolved (for instance as regards equal rights on succession), a notable exception relating to the husband's right to the fruits of his wife's *melog* property (P D 12:1528ff.) A law of 1955 prescribes the status and manner of appointment of rabbinical court *dayyanim* and, except for two variations, its provisions correspond closely to those laid down in the Judges Law, 1953. (As regards two variations see M. Elon, *Ḥakikah Datit . . .,* 47–49.)

THE GENERAL COURTS. In matters of personal status concerning Jewish parties the general courts are also required to decide according to Jewish law, except when a law of the state makes express provision on the matter. As already mentioned, the general courts have jurisdiction in all matters not entrusted to the exclusive jurisdiction of the rabbinical courts. Matters of marriage and divorce may also be pronounced on by the general courts, either when the problem arises incidentally to the matter before the court (for instance in a claim by the wife for maintenance there may arise incidentally thereto the question of the validity of her marriage), or in a matter brought before the Supreme Court sitting as a High Court of Justice. Possibly a rabbinical court and a general court, even though both apply Jewish law, may arrive at entirely different conclusions. Thus, for instance, the general courts first resort to the principles of private international law before applying Jewish law and therefore may recognize a marriage entered into abroad as valid in accordance with the law of the country concerned, even when it is invalid according to Jewish law. In addition the general courts apply only substantive Jewish law and not its laws of evidence and procedure, thus for instance admitting the testimony of the parties themselves and that of their relatives.

LEGISLATIVE PROVISIONS CONTRARY TO JEWISH LAW. Legislation in the area of personal status contrary to Jewish law is reflected in a number of provisions, scattered in various Knesset laws, which confer on the commonly reputed spouse ("wife" as well as "husband") numerous rights. These provisions relate to rights of a social-economic nature (pensions, tenants' protection, and so on), rights, under the Succession Law, and include also the right conferred on a woman to give her child born of the man reputed to be her husband the latter's family name, even without his consent. These rights were held by the Supreme Court to extend to the commonly reputed spouse even though the latter (or even both parties) be validly married to another (except with regard the right of succession, which is only available if, upon the death of one of the parties who have lived together as husband and wife in a common household, neither is then married to another). The explanation that the above enactments were made in order to alleviate the hardship which is sometimes suffered by a couple who are unable to marry on account of Jewish law prohibition (for instance in certain cases of the *agunah*) is indeed weighty and hope may be expressed that the Chief Rabbinate will speedily find solutions to these problems. Nevertheless, it does not seem to justify the institution of the reputed spouse with its threat to the orderly existence of the family unit. This institution is the subject of controversy in Israel society and there are recent indications of a tendency by the Supreme Court to limit its scope (see M. Elon, *Ḥakikah Datit . . .,* 119–54).

"WHO IS A JEW?"—ANSWERED ACCORDING TO JEWISH LAW. In March 1970 an amendment to the Law of Return of 1950 incorporated into this law a most material principle of Jewish law. This law, which ensures for every Jew the right to come to Israel as an *oleh* and automatic citizenship from the moment of his arrival, was amended to define the term "Jew" as a person born of a Jewish mother or converted to Judaism, who is not a member of a different religious faith. This definition, including the latter part, is entirely in accord with Jewish law. A Jew converted to a different faith remains a Jew as regards his personal status and all this entails—such as the need for him to grant a divorce to his Jewish wife—but he is deprived of various religio-social rights and is not numbered as a member of the Jewish community (i.e., he cannot be counted toward *minyan* and so on); for this reason he is also deprived of the rights of a Jew under the Law of Return. The stated definition applies also for purposes of registering an individual's Jewish nationality *(le'om)* in the population register and related documents, including the identity card.

LEGISLATION CONFORMING WITH RITUAL LAW. In addition to the already mentioned cases, Israel law is also based on the *halakhah*—in the wide sense of the term—in a number of different matters. Thus in 1948 the Provisional Council of State enacted that the supply of *kasher* food be ensured to all Jewish soldiers of the Defense Army of Israel; a law of 1962 prohibits the raising, keeping, or slaughtering **109** of pigs in Israel except in specified areas (populated mainly by non-Jews) and for certain other limited purposes; the provisions of the Law and Administration Ordinance of 1948 (as amended) lay down that the Sabbath and the Jewish festivals shall be prescribed days of rest in the state (but do not prohibit labor on such days, such matters being ordered in certain respects in the Hours of Work and Rest Law of 1951) and allows non-Jews the right to observe their own Sabbath and festivals as days of rest.

The "Unofficial" Application of Jewish Law in the State. INDEPENDENCE OF THE ISRAEL LEGAL SYSTEM. As already mentioned, Jewish law is reserved no official place in the Israel legal system save in matters of personal status. The proposal (made by P. Daikan on the eve of the state's establishment and subsequently raised again by others) that Israel law be freed from its independence on the English common law and principles of equity and that Jewish law be resorted to in any case of lacuna in the law of the state (see above, Art. 46 of the Palestine Order in Council) was not accepted. Until the present time there is to be found in two Laws only, the Succession Law of 1965 and the Land Law of 1969, a provision (entitled "Autarky of this Law") which excludes the operation of the aforementioned article 46 in all matters with which the relevant law is concerned. None of the other laws so far passed by the Knesset proclaims its own independent operation. To some extent such independence has been established in the case law in consequence of decisions by the Supreme Court to the effect that the post-1948 English case law does not have binding force in Israel law as does that of the pre-1948 period, and even reliance on the pre-1948 English case law is also gradually diminishing.

LEGISLATION BASED ON JEWISH LAW PRINCIPLES. In some measure law in the State of Israel follows the principles of Jewish law even in areas where the latter system has not officially been rendered applicable. In the introduction to a draft bill for one of the early comprehensive laws there were set out the general legislative guidelines adopted for the entire area of the civil law. The legislative policy thus enunciated assigned to Jewish law the status of "the main but not the only or binding source" and enumerated the existing legal and factual position in Israel as well as the laws of other countries as additional sources (Draft Bill for a Succession Law, published by the Ministry of Justice in 1952). To some extent this policy has been adhered to in practice and some of the matters enacted in accordance with the principles of Jewish law are the following: the possibility of separate ownership of dwellings in a cooperative house; the prohibition of delay in the payment of wages; the right of the dismissed employee to severance pay; the legal arrangement concerning imprisonment for debt; the laws of bailment, and so on. Particular reliance on Jewish law is to be found in the provisions of various Knesset laws in the area of family law, relating among others to the following matters: the duty of a person to maintain, besides his wife and children, also his other relatives (on the Jewish law principle of obliging a person to uphold the *mitzvah* of *zedakah*) in matters of guardianship that the minor's own good is the primary consideration and that "the court is the father of all orphans" and a complete departure—expressed in various provisions—from the Roman law concept of *patria potestas;* in matters of succession Jewish law is followed in the conferment of equal rights on all children of the deceased whether born in or out of wedlock, in the solution provided to the problem which arises in the case of commorientes, in acceptance of the Jewish law institution of a *shekhiv mera* will and in the provision made for maintenance out of the estate of the deceased.

LEGISLATION CONTRARY TO JEWISH LAW. In contrast, there are Knesset laws containing provisions which are—without any real justification—contrary to the position taken by Jewish law. Some of the matters so enacted are the following: the right of the creditor to turn directly to the surety even without initial agreement to this effect; the right of a party to plead prescription of a claim along 111 with an admission as to the existence of the debt; the automatic administration of an oath to all witnesses whereas Jewish law leaves the matter to the discretion of the court.

JEWISH LAW IN THE CASE LAW OF THE GENERAL COURTS. The decisions of the courts, particularly of the Supreme Court, represent a further channel through which the influence of Jewish law is brought to bear on the Israel legal system. In numerous decisions of the Supreme Court diverse legal matters have been dealt with by way of a comparison between the position under the general law and Jewish law respectively, the two systems sometimes leading the judges to the same conclusion and sometimes otherwise. In some cases Jewish law has been quoted for the purpose of construing legal terms and definitions and on occasion Jewish law has constituted the primary legal source relied on by the Supreme Court, even in areas in which Jewish law is not expressly rendered applicable. This integration of Jewish law through the case law of the general courts is of great practical significance from the aspect of the confrontation between Jewish law and the legal problems that have arisen before the courts in the 1950s and 1960s.

JEWISH LAW IN THE CASE LAW OF THE RABBINICAL COURTS. A noteworthy phenomenon is the existence of a proliferous case law of the rabbinical courts, in diverse areas of the civil law, in matters coming before these courts as arbitral bodies. Some 30% of the judgments of these courts published since the middle of the 1960s deal with matters unrelated to personal status and concern, for instance, labor law, contracts, copyright, partnership, pledge, administrative law, and so on. These offer an instructive insight into the manner in which concrete questions of everyday life are dealt with in accordance with Jewish law and represent an important contribution to the solution of modern social and economic problems.

Attitudes Toward Jewish Law in the Law of the State. Integration of Jewish law into the legal system of Israel is sometimes opposed because it entails a "secularization" of the *halakhah* since the acceptance by the state of a Jewish law principle does not stem from recognition of the binding validity of such a principle from the religious point of view, but is dictated by purely human and national interests. The argument views that by such integration the Knesset's own binding authority substitutes itself as the source of authority of any Jewish law principle it has adopted, and that neither the Knesset nor the general courts possess the necessary qualifications postulated by the halakhic system for deciding any of its rules. This view is decried by a decisive majority of religious Jewry and its spiritual leaders, who consider that the *halakhah* does not become secularized for the mere reason that the theory of the general law may hold a change to have taken place as regards the basic norm of a particular halakhic rule. It is argued that neither the Knesset nor the courts purport—nor indeed is it possible for them to do so—to decide the *halakhah* within the religious meaning of such activity; that not only is the *halakhah* not prejudiced by its integration into the legal system of the state, but the halakhic system itself commends that the legal order in the Jewish state shall, even if not based on religious faith, correspond with the substance of Jewish law and its principles of justice and equity rather than be founded on other legal systems. For some generations now this middle path has been followed by a decisive majority of religious Jewry, also with regard to other fundamental Jewish values, as with the revived use of the holy tongue in everyday secular life and with the settlement of the holy land even without observance of the religious precepts. The declared attitude of non-observant Jewry also favors the assignment of first priority to the reception of Jewish law principles when these are in keeping with present-day social and economic needs (see, e.g., the statement made in the session of Nov. 29, 1965, by Knesset members belonging to almost all political parties with reference to the Gift Law and Pledge Law Bills (*Divrei ha-Keneset,* v. 44, pp. 24–36)). It should be borne in mind that except in the area of family law the subject matter of 113

Jewish law is generally free of fundamental public dispute of a religious or ideological nature.

The integration of Jewish law into the legal system of Israel is of importance to the former since it has a vital need to contend with the problems of practical everyday life as the only means toward the restoration of its former, almost unbroken, creative and evolutionary function, and this in its natural environment—the Jewish state and its legal system. Such an integration of Jewish law is no less important for the legal system of the state. Israel legislation is of an eclectic nature, the legislator choosing as he sees fit from many different legal systems. There is well-founded apprehension that this must necessarily result in a lack of homogeneity and lead to contradictions in Israel law due to the absence of a common axis around which the entire legal structure may revolve. A legal system so constructed moreover lacks roots and a past. If, as the revival of Hebrew proved, a people's language has to lean on history and foundations, then a priori a people's legal system requires roots and a past on which to draw for sustenance and growth. The absence of these requisites in Israel law accounts for the large number of Supreme Court decisions evidencing resort to numerous legal systems in a search for solutions to legal problems. The appointed way for the emerging legal system of the Jewish state to take root, to find the common denominator for its laws as well as the homogeneity it requires, is for it to become linked and integrated in the proper way with historical Jewish legal thinking and creativity.

Modes of Integration. Achievement of the desired integration of Jewish law with the Israel legal system demands strict observance of the rule that in all legislative activity preference be given to every principle of Jewish law which is in keeping with the existing social and economic exigencies. It is also necessary to ensure that all principles of Jewish law adopted in the laws of the state shall be construed within the spirit of the Jewish sources of law from which they were derived. Finally, it is necessary to lay down a "Jewish version" of the controversial Article 46, to the effect that the Jewish sources of law shall be resorted to in the event of any lacuna in the existing law. The decisions of the Supreme Court and of the rabbinical courts in matters involving Jewish law—not only in the area of personal status but in all its different fields—and a long series of varied research studies undertaken in recent years, point to the fact that it is within the power of Jewish law to contend successfully with the overall range of new problems that arise. In addition, Jewish law occupies a substantial part of the law faculty study curriculum at different universities in Israel and to the new generation of Israel lawyers and jurists Jewish law is no longer a remote and unfamiliar subject. Accelerated research activity in the different fields of Jewish law and the preparation of an auxiliary literature to facilitate study of and resort to the latter will be invaluable aids to the process of integrating the legal system of the State of Israel and Jewish law.

3 THE SHARIʿA (MUSLIM LAW)

Upon the severance of Palestine from the Ottoman Empire, the country ceased to be a territory under Muslim sovereignty in which the Shariʿa reigned, theoretically supreme, over all spheres of life and society. In the circumstances which combined to bring about the establishment of the State of Israel, the Muslims turned from a majority into a minority with all the attendant legal and political implications. Their communal organization from Mandatory times, once headed by Ḥājj Amīn al-Husseinī, who had wielded unprecedentedly wide powers as mufti of Jerusalem and president of the Supreme Muslim Council, was completely destroyed: the members of the Council and the Shariʿa élite left the country; the religious-legal system, the waqf administration and communal, educational, welfare and health institutions crumbled and ceased to exist.

The Government of Israel proceeded to rehabilitate the organization of the Muslim community (see above Muslims). The religious-legal system was reconstituted: Shariʿa Courts of First Instance and a Court of Appeal were set up. These courts have very wide powers compared with those of the Rabbinical and Christian courts: exclusive jurisdiction in almost all matters of personal status and waqf. The qadis, selected by a special committee with a Muslim majority, are appointed by the President of the State: they must make a declaration of allegiance to the state and dispense justice in accordance with its laws.

Far-reaching reforms, in the spirit of modern Arab legislation, were carried out in the administration of the

Muslim waqf and in the actual institution of the waqf as far as its administrators were absentees. The Absentees' Property (Release and Use of Endowment Property) Law, 5725–1965, abolished the family (*dhurī*) waqf completely in order that the property might be given into the full ownership of the beneficiaries; most of the restrictions on the transfer of waqf property and the use of its income were abolished with regard to waqf *khayrī,* which is destined for public purposes, such as worship, charity, and education: the property, viz., holy places, such as mosques and cemeteries, and their secular appurtenances, such as shops of which the income is used for the maintenance of the holy places and of communal institutions, was to be released to boards of Muslim trustees set up in several towns for its independent administration. The implementation of the Law is in progress.

Religious services, i.e., matters of worship and religious education, have become the responsibility of the state: the state supports Muslim religious functionaries and assists in the establishment of mosques and educational, welfare, and health institutions. Muslim children are given religious

The qadi, Sheikh Hasan Emir al-Ḥabash, officiating in the Muslim Shariʿa Court at Ṭayyiba, 1962. Courtesy Government Press Office, Tel Aviv.

instruction within the framework of the state school curriculum. The Government has frequently declared its readiness to enable Muslims to fulfill the duty of the *hajj*, the pilgrimage to the Muslim holy places in Mecca, just as until the Six-Day War it enabled its Christian citizens to visit the Christian holy places in East Jerusalem and Bethlehem. But all its appeals were disregarded by the Arab countries concerned.

The stronghold of the Shari'a in Israel is religious jurisdiction in matters of personal status, which are closely bound up with religion. The adaptation of the family law of all religious communities in Israel to the changing requirements of society appears to be first and foremost the task of parliament, whose approach to this matter is, of course, different, as to both the social and the religious norm, from that of parliaments in Muslim countries. The Knesset is guided by a desire to equalize women with men as to every legal act and to abolish all discrimination against women resulting from religious law. To be sure, it could not adopt the technique usual in Arab countries of investing reforms with the character of an internal overhaul of Islamic law by inserting elements of the manifold Islamic legal heritage into secular legislation.

The Knesset has interfered in many matters in the domain of family law, but it has done so with important reservations. Its enactments are not to effect any prohibition or permission regarding marriage and divorce; in this sensitive area, it preferred procedural provisions and penal sanctions to substantive provisions (as, e.g., in the matter of the minimum marriage age, the prohibition of divorce against the wife's will, and the prohibition of polygamy), and in matters in which provisions superseding religious law have been enacted, the parties are left free—with certain reservations—to litigate under the latter. Thus, in the sphere of personal law, Israel has two systems, a religious one and a secular one, based on totally different norms.

Most qadis in Israel exercise their powers as men of law,

in the absence of muftis, to adapt the law of personal status to the requirements of contemporary society. They are guided by a social motive, *maṣlaḥa*, and by the principle that innovations are permitted as far as no express prohibition against them is contained in the material sources of Islamic law. Their jurisprudence is characterized by an ambivalent approach. They generally interpret the law in strict adherence to the *taqlīd*, the consolidated doctrine, of the Ḥanafī school. Moreover, some qadis are so zealous for that school as deliberately to refrain from applying provisions of the Ottoman Family Rights Law which conflict with it.

On the other hand, there are many decisions not in accordance with the strict religious-legal norm. To avoid clashing with religious law, the qadis use their personal authority, sometimes with the aid of go-betweens, to bring about an amicable settlement between the parties, and give the compromise arrived at the effect of a judgment; this method does not involve the application of the Shariʿa. But there are qadis who in their liberal interpretation of the law do not hesitate to deviate from the Ḥanafī school. Particularly impressive is the application of the Shariʿa to the Israel Bedouin, who only recently came under Shariʿa jurisdiction. Some qadis do not apply the law to the Bedouin very strictly but compromise with their customs, knowing this to be the way to win them for the Shariʿa and ultimately to bring them wholly within its orbit.

The qadis' attitude toward secular legislation specifically relating to religious courts is also ambivalent. Not all of them are sufficiently alive to the Knesset's reforms in matters such as marriages of minors, polygamy, divorce against the wife's will, and succession; most of them make no use of the wide discretion given them by the Knesset as to permitting the divorce of one's wife, and regard themselves as bound by Shariʿa norms in these matters. Permission is granted almost automatically, or the divorce is confirmed *ex post facto* as far as it is valid according to Islamic law. Contrary to the Knesset's expectations, the 119 qadis do not recognize the bride's being under seventeen as a ground for dissolution of the marriage. By this approach, the qadis unwittingly abet circumvention of the secular law.

However, there are many indications that qadis are responsive to secular legislation. Some rely on it expressly in their decisions, adopt its principles even where this is contrary to Islamic law, as in regard to the status of women as natural guardians of their children. Some display a keen awareness of the ban on divorce against the wife's will and on polygamy, warn against contravention of the law and, where it has been contravened, point out to the plaintiff wife that she may bring a criminal charge against her husband. Sometimes qadis find themselves in a moral dilemma when religious and secular law clash. Their perplexity is reflected in the simultaneous application of elements of both legal systems in spite of the wide chasm between them. There are those who welcome the ban on polygamy and even find support for it in the Koran and modernist interpretation, and on the other hand, show concern for the validity of Islamic law in this matter and find a social justification for it.

This ambivalent approach has an ideological basis. The qadis are not opposed to Knesset interference in matters of personal status so long as it involves no encroachment upon the Shari'a. Some would even welcome further reforms of a procedural or penal character. Some believe that secular penal sanctions can be used to give teeth to Shari'a norms in matters of marriage and divorce which at present depend on ineffectual ethical sanctions. There are even qadis who do not shrink from calling for secular legislation of an explicity substantive character. In sum, it seems that the qadis have made an important contribution to the adaptation of family law to the requirements of a modern society. The progressive attitude of some of them is revealed also in respect of other matters, such as family planning and birth control, autopsies and transplants (including heart transplants).

120

Part Three:

JEWISH RELIGIOUS INSTITUTIONS

1 RABBINATE

The rabbinate and the various functions of the rabbi in modern Israel differ fundamentally from their counterparts in any other part of the Jewish world, whether ancient or modern. A number of factors have contributed toward this unique state of affairs. In the first place there is the law of the State of Israel which establishes the *halakhah* as state law in all matters affecting personal status, which includes

Heikhal Shlomo, seat of the Israel Chief Rabbinate.
Courtesy Government Press Office, Tel Aviv.

marriage, divorce, legitimacy, and conversion and affords the rabbinical courts the status of civil courts of law within that wide sphere. This, coupled with the fact that the Ministry of Religious Affairs was, apart from one brief interregnum, the prerogative of the (Orthodox) National Religious Party, has had the effect of making Orthodox Judaism to all intents and purposes the "established church" of the state, to the virtual exclusion of other religious trends in Judaism, Conservative and Reform, which have only a handful of congregations, mostly composed of recently arrived immigrants belonging to those trends in the countries of their origin.

A second factor determining the complexion and the functions of the rabbinate is the establishment of the twin Orthodox chief rabbinate (Ashkenazi and Sephardi) which are state appointments, and similar twin chief rabbinates in

Electoral assembly for the Chief Rabbinate. Seated in the front row (left to right) are Rabbi Ovadiah Yosef and Rabbi Shlomo Goren, elected Sephardi and Ashkenazi chief rabbis respectively and the two incumbents Rabbi Isaac Nissim and Rabbi Isser Yehuda Unterman. (G. P. O., Tel Aviv) 123

Abraham Isaac Kook speaking at the laying of the corner-stone of the Keneset Israel quarter in Jerusalem, 1925. Courtesy Jerusalem Municipality Historical Archives. Photo Ben Dov, Jerusalem.

Ben-Zion Meir Ḥai Ouziel, Sephardi chief rabbi of Israel 1939–53. Photo K. Weiss, Jerusalem.

Jacob Meir, Sephardi chief
rabbi of Ereẓ Israel. Courtesy Jerusalem Municipality
Historical Archives. Photo
Ben Dov, Jerusalem.

Isaac Herzog, first Ashkenazi chief rabbi of the State
of Israel. Courtesy Central Zionist Archives, Jerusalem.

the larger cities. These local rabbinates and chief rabbinates are administered by the local religious councils, which are nominated through a complicated system of political party representation and the Ministry of Religious Affairs, and it is to all intents controlled by the ministry. These councils consist of Orthodox Jews. All appointments of rabbis must be confirmed by the chief rabbis and the Ministry of Religious Affairs.

A third factor is the fact that almost without exception the *rashei yeshivot,* who exercise a powerful influence in Israel, as well as the other rabbis who belong to the Agudat Israel (to which the *rashei yeshivot* also mostly belong), regard the National Religious Party and the chief rabbis who owe their appointments to their support as tending toward heterodoxy, a charge which they are at great pains to disprove or dispel. As a result, they are unduly apprehensive of any move which might be regarded as progressive or "reform." To these considerations must be added two others. The Ashkenazi rabbinate continues wholly the tradition of the classical Eastern European rabbinate, and the new incumbents to the rabbinate are wholly the products of the yeshivot, while the Sephardi rabbinate equally continues in their old traditions. Lastly, the synagogue in Israel is, with only a handful of exceptions, not a congregational entity with fixed membership but a place for worship and study.

All these factors add up to the distinctive features of the rabbinate and the functions of the rabbis in Israel. Next to the chief rabbis the hierarchy consists of the *dayyanim* of the Supreme Bet Din of Appeal, followed by the *dayyanim* of the district courts. They are classified as civil judges with the emoluments and privileges of judges, and their functions are wholly judicial and not pastoral. Next in importance, and in receipt of salaries from the religious councils, are a host of rabbis who act as religious functionaries with specific and limited duties such as inspection of *kashrut,* of *mikva'ot,* of the *eruv,* of the adherence to the various agricultural laws, etc. They also, by nature of their functions, perform no pastoral duties. Next in the scale come district rabbis, also appointed by the religious councils. In theory they are charged with the welfare of the community within the district over which they have been appointed, but with few exceptions they regard their position as a sinecure. Lowest on the scale come, what in theory is the nearest approach to the Western rabbi, the rabbi of a synagogue. In the absence of a regularly constituted congregation, however, and with no official source of income, they are financially the least rewarded. Few synagogues pay anything approaching a living wage to these rabbis. They mostly depend upon one of the other rabbinic functions referred to for their livelihood, and their appointments largely commence as de facto ones which sometimes develop into uneasy de jure ones. In the absence of the congregational unit with its duly paid-up membership, and the consequent lack of personal bond between rabbi and worshiper, there is nothing in the rabbinate in Israel which approaches the pastoral aspect of the work of the modern rabbi. Marriages are performed by duly appointed officials of the local religious councils, funerals by the various *hevra kaddisha* organizations. Visiting the sick is not regarded as the function of the rabbi of a synagogue; cultural activities apart from the *shi'urim* in rabbinics are undertaken by other agencies, as is youth work and philanthropic activity. The virtual nonexistence of regular preaching should be noted.

The cumulative effect of this situation is that the Western-trained rabbi even of Orthodox Jewry finds it hard to find a place in the rabbinate in Israel. Of all those who have immigrated few have been appointed to a rabbinical position in Israel, and most find their livelihood in other spheres.

2 SYNAGOGUES

Because of the fact that it is a "Jewish" country, many of the various functions performed by the synagogue in other countries are provided in Israel by other agencies, often governmental. The nature of the country also obviates the need to affiliate with a synagogue to express one's Jewish identity. Education, including religious, is the concern of the state; burial is the concern of independent burial societies; *kashrut* is supervised and arranged by the Rabbinate, at its different levels, which institution is financed by the government and independent of the synagogue. Thus, in the Jewish country, a paradoxical situation has arisen; one would have thought that the synagogue would flourish and expand its influence, when in fact it has become little more than a house of prayer. The population, even the religious section of it, finds its expression within other frameworks (see above Religious Life).

While the main function of synagogues in Israel is to serve as places of worship, many also organize daily or weekly lectures or classes for their congregants. A vast variety of synagogue services can be found throughout the country, each community of the Diaspora bringing to Israel its own customs and manners. The multiplicity of traditions presents a peculiar problem for the army, since there is no possibility of establishing synagogues suited to the specific customs of diverse communities in every military camp and base. Nor can the army "melting pot" permit soldiers to be divided in prayer. Thus, by force of circumstances, a uniform type of synagogue has emerged, encouraged also by the way in which children from different communities join in prayer and study at religious schools and *yeshivot*.

This pattern has been followed by the younger generation in civilian life, and about 300 synagogues of a unified type have been set up, combining elements from the

Ark of the Law in the Ashkenazi Ari Synagogue in Safed, named after Rabbi Isaac Luria. Originally built at the end of the 16th century, the synagogue was reconstructed after the earthquake of 1837. Courtesy Government Press Office, Tel Aviv.

The Yohanan ben Zakkai Sefardi Synagogue, one of a complex of four synagogues in the Old City of Jerusalem destroyed by the Jordanians in 1948 and reconstructed in 1972. (G. P. O., Tel Aviv)

rituals of *Ḥasidim* and *Mitnaggedim,* and from Ashkenazim and Sephardim. Before the establishment of the state, there were few distinguished synagogue buildings in the country. Baron Edmond de Rothschild erected a synagogue in every settlement that he endowed, and the buildings are still to be seen in Zikhron Ya'akov, Rishon le-Zion, Mazkeret Batyah, and elsewhere. The old *yishuv* in Safed, Tiberias, and Hebron had a number of poor synagogue buildings. The Jewish Quarter of Old Jerusalem contained 58 synagogues which had served the Sephardi and Ashkenazi communities from the time when Naḥmanides[14] renewed Jewish life in Jerusalem after the Crusades. Among them was the Sephardi Great Synagogue of Rabban Johanan ben Zakkai, which included four synagogues in a single large block. The largest synagogue of the Ashkenazi

[14] Spanish rabbi and scholar (1194–1270)

community was called the Ḥurvah ("Ruin"), since it was built on the ruins of the House of Study of Rabbi Judah Hasid. Other notable synagogues were the Bet El synagogue of the kabbalists and the Tiferet Israel synagogue, also called Nisan Bak, after its founder. The oldest synagogue was that of the Karaites, ascribed to the tenth or eleventh century. During and after the 1948 War of Independence, 55 of these synagogues were destroyed by the Arabs, but some others (Ramban, Ḥabad and Rabban Johanan ben Zakkai) were restored after the liberation of the Old City in June, 1967.

During the British Mandate (1917–48) synagogue building proceeded slowly, principally in the larger cities and with the financial assistance of the local community. Thus in 1923–24 the Great Synagogue and the Sephardi Synagogue Ohel Mo'ed in Tel Aviv, and Yeshurun in Jerusalem, were established, and in the 1930s the Central Synagogue of Haifa was founded. At the time of the establishment of the state in 1948 there were about 800 synagogues of all kinds throughout the country, serving a Jewish population of 650,000. The rapid growth of immigrant housing and the development of townships necessitated new synagogues, particularly where there were liturgical and ritual differences. New buildings were also erected to replace the provisional structures in the veteran religious settlements.

In 1970 there were about 6,000 synagogues. These new synagogues were jointly financed by the Ministry for Religious Affairs, the Ministry of Housing, the Jewish Agency, the Jewish Restitution Successor Organization, the Silverman Fund, the Wolfson Trust, and other agencies. The complete interior furnishing of nine synagogues from Jewish communities destroyed during World War II, and 28 arks from old synagogues in Italy, were transferred to Israel and reconstructed in various places throughout the country. The first of these came in 1952 from Coneglia, near Venice, and was reestablished as

The Tiferet Israel Synagogue in the Old City, dedicated in 1865 and universally known by the name of Nisan Bak. Courtesy Keren Hayesod, United Israel Appeal, Jerusalem.

the Synagogue of *Benei Roma* in Jerusalem. Others came from Mantua, Padua, and Florence.

There is no distinctive form of synagogue architecture in Israel. Some local congregations have, however, evolved an architecture suited to their specific needs or exploiting local building materials—eucalyptus, olive wood, and marble from the Negev and Galilee. A modern Israel style seems to be emerging gradually, one of its features being the exterior *menorah* (candelabra), which epitomizes the light of the Torah and is also the emblem of the State of Israel. The synagogue interiors usually conform to the pattern of the congregation's place of origin, and contain carpets and rugs and European or oriental furniture. There is some new artistic expression in adornments by famous artists, such as Marc Chagall's stained-glass windows at the Hadassah Medical Center Synagogue in Jerusalem. The vast majority of synagogues in Israel are Orthodox, and the traditional partition between the main hall and the women's gallery (*Meḥizah*) prevails in all of them, with variations as to the form and height of the grate or curtain. The *bimah* (platform) is situated in the middle of the synagogue, while the *ammud* (precentor's lectern) is close to the ark at the front wall. Sephardi synagogues, however, have no lecterns. Low seating is generally provided around the walls of the room and the almemar is always in the center. Occasionally a special chair, of Moses or Elijah, is attached high up on the wall. Prayers are usually led by congregants although in some of the modern Sephardi synagogues in Israel salaried officials are employed. In 1963, a Union of Israel Synagogues, embracing all the Orthodox synagogues, was established by Hechal Shlomo, Jerusalem. In 1970 there were six Conservative and eight Reform synagogues in Israel, many of them using provisional premises. The most prominent of these is the Hebrew Union College's synagogue in Jerusalem. The Karaites, who number about 10,000, have their own houses of prayer. They are concentrated mainly in Ramleh, but are also to be found in Ashdod, Ofakim, Beersheba, Rannen, Bat Yam, Kiryat Gat, Kiryat Malakhi, Yavneh, Mevasseret Zion, Jerusalem, Maẓli'aḥ, Beth-Shemesh, and Acre.

3 YESHIVOT

Israel became the greatest and most important center of yeshivot, having in 1970 the greatest number of yeshivot and students since the talmudic era. In Israel there were also to be found the greatest number of diversified types of yeshivot each of which had a character of its own. (1) The yeshivot of the old *yishuv,* the oldest in the country, pertained to the very structure of this *yishuv* and were to a great degree connected with the *kolelim* and with the system of the *ḥalukkah.* They provided talmudic education for large numbers. Most of the students were of mature age, some continuing their study during their whole lifetime. Generally speaking about 20 to 30 men, mostly married, were concentrated in such a yeshivah and they received a minimal material support. In most of these yeshivot the system of study was undefined. The larger yeshivot of this type, with hundreds of students (like Eẓ Ḥayyim, or Ḥayyei Olam in Jerusalem), had a character similar to that of the ordinary large yeshivot, and tuition was given in Yiddish. With this type should be connected a number of yeshivot that study Kabbalah. (2) The Sephardi yeshivot, the largest and oldest of which was Porat Yosef in Jerusalem, still followed the old Sephardi pattern of study, strong stress being placed on the preparation of religious functions for oriental communities all over the world. (3) The central yeshivot, removed from Eastern Europe to Israel (like Slobodka-Hebron), or whose heads reestablished them with the same composition and names, the same applying to the large ḥasidic yeshivot transferred from their center in

Poland. An important aspect of yeshivot in Israel were the *kolelim* which developed greatly and in which the young men continued their studies after marriage and at a higher level. These *kolelim* were dependent on the large yeshivot and were an important factor in raising the level of studies in the whole yeshivah. From these *kolelim*, unlike those of the old *yishuv*, the scholars passed after five to ten years to serve as rabbis, *dayyanim*, or teachers at yeshivot. Some of them worked at preparing manuscripts of rabbinic works for publication, in a scientific manner. A number (like Merkaz ha-Rav and Kol Torah in Jerusalem) gave all the tuition in Hebrew but in most the official *shi'ur* was still given in Yiddish, even though most of the learning was conducted in Hebrew.

Another very important change was the attempt to combine secular studies within the framework of the classical yeshivah and at a parallel standard. The idea first arose among German Orthodoxy by scholars such as S. R. Hirsch, as an expression of the aims of *Torah im Derekh Ereẓ* ("Jewish with secular learning"), but without any connection with the activity and programs of Orthodox

The Porat Yosef Yeshivah in the Bukharan quarter of Jerusalem, 1951. Photo K. Weiss, Jerusalem.

proponents of the Wissenschaft des Judentums or the various types of rabbinical seminary. Chiefly in Erez Israel—and later in the State of Israel—numerous new types of yeshivah were created which combined the classical learning within their compass with various and diversified forms of secular studies organized according to the pattern of the different general schools and subject to the general directions, inspection, and examinations of the state Department of Education. The essence of the attempt and the most successful were the *yeshivot tikhoniyyot* ("high school yeshivot") which finally emerged as the minor yeshivah in which the instruction during the first half of the day was devoted to Talmud with secondary school studies in the afternoon. The talmudic studies in these yeshivot were dominated by the Lithuanian system of study. The success of the attempt brought about its diversification into combinations of "vocational yeshivot" and "agricultural yeshivot," etc. Many minor yeshivot and *yeshivot tikhoniyyot* existed in Israel, and most of the pupils continued in the large yeshivot. The first yeshivah that began to move in this direction was the yeshivah of Ha-Yishuv he-Ḥadash

The *bet ha-midrash* of the Kol Torah Yeshivah, Bayit va-Gan, Jerusalem, 1970. Photo K. Weiss, Jerusalem.

(the "new settlement") in Tel Aviv, established by Rabbi M. A. Amiel, in which only the evening hours were devoted to secular studies and a fifth year was added to make it possible for the students to take the state matriculation examination. A greater, more direct influence was achieved by the yeshivah of the Benei Akiva movement in Kefar ha-Ro'eh, which became the pattern for about 20 other yeshivot. These yeshivot competed with the religious grammar schools and even encroached upon them. From the teaching standpoint, the two parts, the sacred and the secular, remained uncombined but side by side, but educationally a successful combination was achieved. The number of students in the lower yeshivot was about 10,000 in 1970, about half of them in the *tikhoniyyot*.

On the establishment of the State of Israel the heads of the yeshivot came to an agreement with the Ministry of Defense that their students would be exempt from military service, on grounds of recognition of the duty to help in the spiritual rebuilding of Judaism after the Holocaust. This agreement had no legal validity but was an ad hoc arrangement according to which the yeshivah students were regarded as receiving deferment for the duration of their studies. The arrangement was viewed with mixed feelings by the public, even including religious circles, and many yeshivah students interrupted their studies in order to do their military service. In a number of yeshivot there existed various arrangements that combined yeshivah studies with active service, particularly in the framework of Naḥal.

Most yeshivot in Israel were administratively combined under a loose roof organization, called Va'ad ha-Yeshivot; about ten yeshivot with around 500 students were connected with the Iḥud ha-Yeshivot of the Neturei Karta. Few yeshivot were definitely associated with a specific religious political party, but most of their heads and students were close to Agudat Israel and supported it. Those yeshivot closer to the National Religious Party served as a factor inclining their party in a more conservative direction.

Part Four:

HOLY PLACES

Because of its long and rich history, the Land of Israel possesses places holy to the three monotheistic religions, although the term "holy" means something different to each of these religions, Judaism, Christianity, and Islam. While the veneration of these sites by believers is genuine, the authenticity of the sites themselves is sometimes questionable.

1 JEWISH HOLY PLACES

Although there are certain sites in Israel (mostly graves) which are popularly considered to be holy and as such venerated and visited, the notion is almost nonexistent in primary Jewish sources. The Mishnah (Kel. 1:6) states: "There are ten degrees of holiness. The land of Israel is holier than any other land ... in that from it they may bring the *omer*, the firstfruits, and the Two Loaves which they may not bring from any other land. The walled cities are still more holy in that they must send forth the lepers from their midst ... Within the wall [of Jerusalem] is still more holy for there only may they eat the Lesser Holy Things ... The Holy of Holies is still more holy for none may enter therein save only the high priest on the Day of Atonement at the time of the *Avodah*." It seems clear therefore, that holiness, insofar as it can be applied to places, is measured according to the laws and *mitzvot* applying to the place in question, and not according to what may once have happened there or to who might be buried there. As a Christian theologian put it:

"For Christians and Muslims that term [sacred sites] is an adequate expression of what matters. Here are sacred places, hallowed by the most holy events, here are the places for pilgrimage, the very focus of highest devotion . . . But Judaism is different . . . The sites sacred to Judaism have no shrines. Its religion is not tied to 'sites' but to the land, not to what happened in Jerusalem but to Jerusalem itself" (K. Stendahl, in: *Harvard Divinity Bulletin* (Autumn 1967), 7).

However, in the course of time, and perhaps under non-Jewish influences, Jews came to regard some places as being holy and prayer offered there as more efficacious than at other places. The most venerated of these places is the Western Wall, a relic of the Temple of Herod[15]. While Jews were allowed to pray there by the Muslim authorities and, in the modern period, by the British mandatory government, severe restrictions were placed on their presence there, especially after the riots in 1929. From 1948 the Wall, being in the sector of the city occupied by Jordan, was not accessible to Jews, notwithstanding a clause in the armistice agreement to the contrary. With the reunification of the city in 1967 the Wall became the central attraction for Jewish pilgrims. Prayer services are held there daily from sunrise to nightfall and people come at all times for meditation. While there is a popular custom of inserting slips of paper bearing petitions in the cracks of the Wall, some people refrain from even touching it because of its holiness. The Temple site itself is even more holy, but Jewish religious law forbids entry into its precincts, as all people are considered ritually unclean because of the impurity of touching dead persons (Num. 19:11–22).

The other holy places are all graves of biblical figures or famous rabbis and pious men from the mishnaic period until today. In Jerusalem the Mount of Olives was a center of pilgrimage, perhaps because of its proximity to the

The alleged tomb of King David on Mount Zion in Jerusalem.
Courtesy Government Press Office, Tel Aviv.

Temple site or because of the prophecy that on the Day of
the Lord (i.e., the Day of Resurrection according to the oral
tradition): "His feet shall stand upon the Mount of Olives"
(Zech. 14:4). The mount has served as a general burial
ground for many centuries and according to tradition (II
Chron. 24:20f.) the prophet Zechariah is buried at its foot.

The traditional tomb of Rachel, near Bethlehem, 1913. Courtesy
New York State Education Department.

Also in Jerusalem is the tomb of King David on Mount
Zion, which is certainly spurious. This fact did not,
however, prevent it from being a popular focus for
pilgrimage especially during the period when the Western
Wall was not accessible. The grave of Simeon the Just[16] in
Jerusalem is also popular and, to some degree, serves as a
substitute for that of Simeon b. Yoḥai[17] in Meron.

The most important grave is that of the patriarchs
in Hebron. This shrine, known in the Bible as the cave of
the Machpelah, is housed in a building with Herodian
walls, which was converted in its last phase into a mosque
and was therefore inaccessible to both Jews and Christians
for centuries. "Infidels" were allowed to ascend to the
seventh step of the entrance, but there is evidence that in the
late Middle Ages there was a synagogue next to the mosque.
After 1967 this site became a focus for pilgrimage and
special hours are set aside for non-Muslim visitors. The

[16] High priest in the time of Alexander the Great
[17] Tanna (mid. 2nd cent. C.E.)

traditional tomb of Rachel is near Bethlehem, while that of her son Joseph is in Shechem. In Haifa the cave of Elijah, where according to tradition the prophet hid, is considered holy and a place for pilgrimage.

Most of the graves visited by pilgrims are in Galilee, because most of the rabbis of the Talmud lived and taught

Praying in the cave of Elijah the Prophet on Mount Carmel.

Courtesy Government Press Office, Tel Aviv.

there. Particularly important is the town of Meron where Simeon b. Yohai and his son Eleazar are reputedly buried. Extensive popular celebrations take place there on Lag ba-Omer and a kind of cult has grown up around the grave. Hillel and Shammai, among others, are also believed to be buried in Meron. Safed and Tiberias are very important centers for pilgrims to the graves of famous scholars. In the former are the reputed graves of Shemaiah and Avtalion, Phinehas b. Jair, R. Joseph Caro, the kabbalists Isaac Luria, Moses Cordovero, and Solomon Alkabez, as well as many later scholars, saints, and hasidic *zaddikim*. Tiberias was a center of rabbinic activity in talmudic times, and the graves of the talmudic rabbis Akiva, Meir, Johanan b. Zakkai, Eliezer b. Hyrcanus, Ammi and Assi as well as of Maimonides and Isaiah Horowitz[18] are frequently visited.

Visiting graves of the pious in the Holy Land was considered an act of piety, and was widespread from the early Middle Ages. The custom of visiting graves itself seems to be of old Arabic origin. Nearly all the Jewish travelers who visited Erez Israel mentioned graves in their accounts and, indeed, many travel books outlining itineraries and listing the graves enjoyed wide circulation. A pilgrimage to a holy grave was considered to have therapeutic value and many customs developed for such visits. Candles were lit at the grave; often the supplicants made ceremonial processions around it and prostrated themselves on it. There was—and still is—a widespread custom of placing a small stone or pebble on the grave and some pilgrims take a stone from it when they leave. It is also common practice to leave a written petition at the grave. As early as the beginning of the tenth century the Karaite scholar Sahl b. Mazli'ah complained: "How can I remain silent when some Jews are behaving like idolators? They sit at the graves, sometimes sleeping there at night, and appeal to the dead: 'Oh! Rabbi Yose ha-Gelili! Heal me! Grant me children!' They kindle lights there and offer incense . . .''

Visiting holy graves was considered particularly desirable by the kabbalists of Safed. Isaac Luria, the foremost exponent of that school, is credited with having "revealed" hitherto unknown graves, although the location of most of them is known by oral and earlier written traditions and itineraries. The purpose of such visits seems to have been to commune with the departed saint and absorb some of his qualities. The grave thus served as a point of focus: the recitation of psalms and prayers, as well as meditation and study there, would enable the pilgrim to reach new heights of spirituality.

2 CHRISTIAN HOLY PLACES

There are numerous holy places to be found throughout the country. They are almost all connnected with the life and death of Jesus of Nazareth. During the first two centuries the early Christians expected a rapid end to this present age and had, therefore, little interest in preserving the memory of holy sites. Moreover, as members of a persecuted religion they were unable to make public pilgrimages or erect conspicuous shrines. The story begins, therefore, with the cessation of persecution and the recognition of the Church by Constantine[19](312–337 C.E.). Constantine's mother, Helena, visited the Holy Land seeking traces of the life and death of Jesus. She established the place of his birth in Bethlehem and of his crucifixion and resurrection in Jerusalem. On these sites magnificent churches were built, relics of which are embodied in the churches of the Nativity and of the Holy Sepulcher, though the present structures date from various later periods. Churches were also built in other parts of the country at the sites of various miracles and significant events and in commemoration of important Christian figures. There are several holy places around the Sea of Galilee; Kefar Nahum (Capernaum) was the site of many of Jesus' miracles and is considered sacred, as is the Mount of Beatitudes, the site of the Sermon on the Mount. The miracle of the wine is commemorated at Kafr Kana and that of the fish and the bread at Tabgha. Nazareth is

[19] First Christian emperor of Rome.

Greek Orthodox procession in the Church of the Nativity, Bethlehem. Courtesy Foreign Ministry, Jerusalem.

The Church of Beatitudes traditional site of the Sermon on the Mount, by the Sea of Galilee. Courtesy Government Press Office, Tel Aviv.

regarded as a holy city in that it has a number of churches on holy sites. The site of the baptism on the Jordan River is also considered holy. In Jerusalem the stations of the cross on the Via Dolorosa are points for pilgrimage, as are the Hall of the Last Supper and the Dormition Abbey (where Mary fell into an eternal sleep) on Mount Zion. The Monastery of the Cross is reputedly on the site from which the wood for the cross was taken. The splitting of the Christian world into different sects gradually produced intense rivalry about the use of these shrines. At first there was a good deal of mutual accommodation, but in the 11th century there was a major schism between the eastern (Greek Orthodox) and the Latin (Roman Catholic) churches, and thereafter each struggled to exclude the other from their use. The churches of Georgia, Armenia, Syria, Egypt (the Coptic Church), and Ethiopia also possessed ancient rights in the holy places. After the Arab conquest, legal ownership was claimed by Islam, which retained and regulated the use of shrines of interest for themselves, while selling to Jews or Christians permission to conduct their own worship in those allowed them. The result was continuous and unedifying bribery, and gradually the lesser churches were elbowed out of any central position.

In 1757 the Turkish government established the rights in nine of the most important shrines; this statute, known as the status quo, was confirmed in 1852, guaranteed by the European powers in 1878, and carefully registered by the British in 1929. The only Jewish shrine affected by the status quo was the Western Wall, as access to it involved passage over Muslim property which was claimed as holy to Islam

Consecration of the new Basilica of the Annunciation,
Nazareth, in front of the Grotto of the Annunciation, March 1969.
Courtesy Government Press Office, Tel Aviv.

The crypt of the Benedictine Church of the Dormition on Mount Zion, marking the traditional spot where Mary, mother of Jesus, fell into an eternal sleep. Courtesy Government Press Office, Tel Aviv.

in that Muhammad's steed Burāq was tethered at the top of the wall during the time that the prophet ascended to heaven. In many places the rivalry between the churches was settled by the adoption of different sites to commemorate the same event. There are, thus, two Gardens of Gethsemane (Mark 14:32), two scenes of the Transfiguration (9:2), and so on. The major churches are, however, shared between the sects.

Pope Paul VI praying in the Hall of the Last Supper on Mount Zion during his visit to Jerusalem in 1964. Courtesy Government Press Office, Tel Aviv.

3 MUSLIM HOLY PLACES

The main Muslim holy place in Jerusalem is the complex of buildings known in Arabic as *Ḥaram al-Sharīf* and was erected after the Arab conquest of Jerusalem at various times on the immense platform of the Temple Mount. The site is dominated by the beautiful Dome of the Rock, built by the caliph ʿAbd al-Malik in 72 A.H. (691

The *even shetiyyah* ("foundation stone") over which the Dome of the Rock is built, regarded by Jewish and Islamic tradition as the center of the world. Photo Richard Cleave, Jerusalem.

C.E.). From the rock at the center of the mosque, Muhammad is said to have ascended to heaven *(miʿrāj)*. Also on the platform is the al-Aqṣā Mosque, completed two years later. The name, meaning "furthermost" (from Mecca), is mentioned in the Koran (Sura 17:2) in the description of the prophet's miraculous journey from Mecca *(isrāʾ)*. As with most of the other Muslim holy places in the country, the real origin of the veneration lies in Muhammad's respect for the earlier monotheisms. The tombs of the patriarchs in Hebron and of King David on Mount Zion were both regarded as holy. Nabī Rūbīn at Nahal Sorek is revered as the grave of the biblical Reuben. However, there are some exclusively Muslim graves. Among them are those of Ṣāliḥ, who lived before Muhammad and is mentioned in the Koran, in Ramleh, and, in Herzliyyah, Sayyidunā Ali, a Muslim who fell in the wars against the Crusaders in the 13th century. More curious is Nebi Mūsā (the tomb of Moses), on the road to Jericho, which from the time of Saladin became the scene of an annual pilgrimage dated by the Christian calendar to rival the Easter pilgrimages. Islam also claims a part in the shrines devoted to Mary, the mother of Jesus, and Muslims are entitled to pray in the Church of the Nativity and that of

The Al-Aqṣā Mosque in the Ḥaram al-Sharīf in Jerusalem.
Courtesy Government Press Office, Tel Aviv.

the Tomb of the Virgin outside the eastern wall of Jerusalem.

Other Religions. The holy place of the Samaritans is Mount Gerizim, where, according to their tradition, Abraham bound Isaac, and the Temple should be built. Every year the sacrifice of the paschal lamb takes place there. For the Druze, Nabī Shuʿayb, the grave of Jethro, the father-in-law of Moses, is a main focus for pilgrimage at Kefar Ḥattin. They adore other graves too, e.g., Nabī Sabalān (Heb. Zebulun, one of Jacob's sons), in the Galilee. The Bahai revere the place in Haifa, where Mirza Ali Muhammad is buried. A beautiful shrine has been built there. Near Acre is the grave of Bahāʾ-Allah (after whom that religious movement is called), who was buried in the house in which he lived and died in exile.

4 THE POLITICAL ASPECTS OF THE HOLY PLACES

With the advance throughout the Middle East of the Seljuk Turks in 1071 Christian pilgrimages to the Holy Land were severely hampered. A crusade was called in 1095 in order to free the Holy Sepulcher and safeguard the pilgrimage routes. Jerusalem was finally conquered by the crusaders in 1099 and its shrines were placed under the protection of the Latin ruler, who was proclaimed *advocatus* (defender) of the Holy Sepulcher. The Orthodox Church subsequently lost much of its influence over the control of the holy places, which fell into the hands of the Latin Church. After the fall of Jerusalem to the Turks in 1187 Christian pilgrimages were again suspended, but Richard I of England gained the right of access for Christians to the Holy Sepulcher five years later. This was not sufficient for Innocent III who summoned the unsuccessful Fourth Crusade to the shrines in 1198. By the Treaty of Jaffa in 1229 between Emperor Frederick II and the sultan of Egypt, Jerusalem, Nazareth, and Bethlehem were reopened to pilgrims. With the conquest of the Holy Land by the Ottoman Turks in the 16th century the problem of the holy places took on a new aspect. Political factors of an international nature were introduced. During the four centuries of Ottoman rule (1517–1917) there were many ups and downs in the struggle about the possession of the holy places between the two main divisions of Christianity in the

East: the Latins and the churches united with Rome and the Greek Orthodox Church and its denominational dependents. Greek influence grew after the fall of Byzantium, owing to the fact that the Greeks were then subjects of the Ottoman Empire. Some of them, having attained important offices at the court of Constantinople, had a direct influence upon the affairs of the Christian holy places. It was consequently not by chance that at the same time the Greek Orthodox Brotherhood of the Holy Sepulcher was reorganized and its authority over the holy places was reinforced. The reaction of Western Christianity did not fail to come. Francis I, king of France, stepped in as the protector of the Latin interests in the holy places, and in 1535 negotiated a treaty with Suleiman the Magnificent, which marks the beginning of a new era in regard to the conflicting claims to the holy places. The Greeks reacted in defense of their interests and the balance of the rights in the holy places was shifted several times from the Greeks to the Latins and back. Decisive moments in the history of this struggle were the Capitulations of 1740, which awarded far-reaching rights to the Latins, and the firman of 1757, which reversed the situation in favor of the Orthodox. In the second half of the 18th century, czarist Russia entered the fray in support of the Orthodox. A further important step was the firman given in 1852 by the sultan, 'Abd al Majīd, confirming de facto the situation in existence since 1757. The international importance of the problem of the holy places, however, was emphasized at the Congress of Berlin in 1878. That treaty (art. 62) uses the expression "status quo," which since then has been employed to describe the de facto situation in respect to the holy places. Nevertheless, it has never been possible to define this "status quo," as there have never been exact descriptions of the de jure and de facto conditions of the situation. At the end of World War I, with the defeat of the Ottoman Empire, the League of Nations, with the assent of the principle powers, granted Great Britain the mandate over Palestine (June 24, 1922).   157

According to Article 13 of the mandate, all responsibility "in connection with the holy places and religious buildings or sites in Palestine, including that of preserving existing rights and of guaranteeing access to the holy places, religious buildings and sites, and free access of worship" was placed on the mandatory power. The latter in turn was responsible solely to the League of Nations in "all matters connected therewith." Article 14 required the appointment by the mandatory of a special commission "to study, define, and determine the rights and claims in connection with the holy places and the rights and claims relating to the different religious communities in Palestine." The composition and function of the commission had to be approved by the Council of the League. Thus, the rights of the mandatory power were circumscribed and matters connected with the holy places were under the supervision of the League of Nations. A very general control was indeed acknowledged. This, however, by no means implied territorial internationalization for the better guarantee of the religious aspects of Jerusalem and the holy places.

In 1947 the Trusteeship Council of the United Nations prepared a list of holy places and sites in Palestine, containing 174 names, 80 of which were in the area of Jerusalem and 94 in other parts of the country. When Great Britain declared that it was no longer willing to administer the mandate, the General Assembly of the United Nations on Nov. 29, 1947, adopted Resolution 181/II on the basis of suggestions presented by the United Nations Special Committee on Palestine (UNSCOP). These suggestions called for the partition of Palestine into two states, one Jewish and one Arab, and the internationalization of Jerusalem. The projected plan aimed to withdraw control from the two states over the main holy places in and around Jerusalem and Bethlehem. Throughout the period of 1948 to 1967, the physical internationalization of Jerusalem was rejected by the parties directly concerned: Israel, which had the western part of the Holy City, and Jordan which was in possession of the eastern part. By

April 3, 1949, the date of the armistice agreement between Israel and Jordan, the situation had crystallized. Consequently, the great majority of the holy places and all those to which the "status quo" is applied, remained in Jordanian-held territory (see map). On Dec. 9, 1949, the General Assembly of the United Nations adopted a resolution calling for the internationalization of the entire Jerusalem area and its environs. And later on, the Trusteeship Council adopted a draft statute under which the city was to be constituted a "corpus separatum." More resolutions were adopted in the following years. While the matter was discussed in the international forum, Israel always opposed the scheme of territorial internationalization as being unrealistic and unpracticable. Israel instead suggested a functional internationalization involving an international answerability for freedom of access to the holy places and of worship at them. Following the cease-fire agreement of June 1967, the Holy City was reunified and Bethlehem came under Israel administration; from 1967 all the holy places of the Holy Land were situated in Israel territory. Israel had already enunciated its policy with regard to the holy places when it declared in its Declaration of Independence, "The State ... will safeguard the holy places of all religions." But following the events of June 1967 and Israel's increased responsibility with regard to holy places formerly situated in the Jordanian-held zone, a new pronouncement by the Israel government was felt to be appropriate. At a meeting on June 27, 1967, which included the two chief rabbis, the representatives of the Muslim clergy, and the heads of the Christian communities, the prime minister of Israel, Mr. Levi Eshkol, affirmed that the government of Israel held it to be an essential principle of its policy to safeguard the holy places, emphasizing that the internal administration of their sites and measures to be taken for their management would be left entirely to the spiritual heads concerned. On the same day the Knesset passed the Law for the Protection of the Holy Places, which prescribes that 159 whoever in any way desecrates or violates a holy place is liable to seven years' imprisonment and to a five years' term if he is found guilty of preventing free access to such a place.

5 THE WESTERN WALL

That section of the western supporting wall of the Temple Mount which has remained intact since the destruction of the Second Temple (70 C.E.). It became the most hallowed spot in Jewish religious and national consciousness and tradition by virtue of its proximity to the Western Wall of the Holy of Holies in the Temple, from which, according to numerous sources, the Divine Presence never departed.

This relic of the Temple of Herod became a center for mourning over the destruction of the Temple and Israel's exile, on the one hand, and of religious—and in the 20th century also national—communion with the memory of Israel's former glory and the hope for its restoration, on the other. Because of the former association, it became known in European languages as the "Wailing Wall" (or similar appellations). Most of the Western Wall of the Temple Mount, which was about 1,580 ft. (485 m.) long, is hidden by the buildings adjoining it. The accessible portion of the Wall was (until June 1967) no longer than 91 ft. (28 m.) from the Maḥkama building on the north to the Prophet's Gate (Barclay's Gate below the Moghrabis' Gate) on the south. In front of it ran a stone-paved alley no wider than 10 ft. (3.3 m.) bordered on its west by a slum area, the Moghrabi Quarter, established in the 14th century. The Wall aboveground consisted of 24 rows (layers) of stones of different dressing and decreasing size and age, reaching a total height of 58 ft. (18 m.) with 19 ft. (6 m.) above the level of the Temple Mount. In 1867 excavations revealed that 19 more rows lay buried underground, the lowest being sunk into the natural rock of the Tyropoeon Valley.

In 1968 the ground in front of the Wall was excavated to reveal two of the buried rows of stone, and the Wall then consisted of seven layers of huge, marginally dressed ("Herodian") stones from the Second Temple, above which are four layers of smaller, plainly dressed stones from the Roman (possibly Hadrianic—second century C.E.) or Byzantine periods. The upper stones were constructed from the Arab period (seventh century) onward, but are probably Mamluk. Jewish travelers over the centuries used to marvel at the immense dimensions of the lower stones—average height $3\frac{1}{4}$ ft. (1 m.), and length 10 ft. (3.3 m.), but some as long as 39 ft. (12 m.) and weighing over 100 tons—and believed they were part of Solomon's Temple. They were probably quarried at the Cave of Zedekiah (near the Damascus Gate). In order to withstand the soil pressure of the filling behind the Wall, the rows were laid in a terraced manner, each row being set back a few inches relative to the one beneath it. The Wall thus slants slightly eastward. This factor, the weight of the stones, and the accuracy of the cutting accounts for the unusual stability of the Wall, which, though built without mortar, withstood repeated earthquakes over the centuries.

In Jewish Tradition and History. Since 135 C.E. (the failure of the Bar Kokhba revolt), the prayers of Israel both in Erez Israel and throughout the Diaspora were directed toward the site of the destroyed Temple. The Temple itself, as well as all the structures on the Temple Mount, were completely effaced, and thus the walls, the only remnants of the Temple Mount, became endeared to the Jews. It cannot be determined with certainty from what point prayers were offered just at this particular section of the Western Wall. Midrashic sources speak of "the Western Wall of the Temple" or of "the Western Gate," from which the Divine Presence never moves, which was not destroyed and never will be destroyed (Ex. R. 2:2; Num. R. 11:2, etc.). It seems probable, however, that the rabbis were referring to the Western Wall of the Holy of Holies and that its indestructibility is symbolic rather than actual, since that wall was in fact destroyed. The notion of the ever-present *Shekhinah* therefore became associated with the Western Wall (of the Temple Mount). Sources about the Jews in Jerusalem up to the 16th century note their attachment to the site of the Holy Place, but the Western Wall is not referred to specifically. In the geonic period the place of assembly and prayer of Jews was on the Mount of Olives. The scroll of Ahimaaz (11th century) mentions "a synagogue by the side of the Western Wall." Benjamin of Tudela[22] (12th century) mentions the Western Wall, together with "the Mercy Gate" (which is in the eastern wall of the Temple Mount). The Western Wall is not mentioned at all by Naḥmanides (13th century) in his detailed account of the Temple site in 1267 nor in the report of Estori ha-Parḥi[23] (14th century). It does not figure even in descriptions of Jerusalem in Jewish sources of the 15th century (e.g., Meshullam of Volterra[24], Obadiah of Bertinoro[25], etc.). The name Western Wall, used by Obadiah, refers—as can be inferred from the context—to the southwestern corner of the wall, and there is no hint that there was a place of Jewish worship there.

The Western Wall became a permanent feature in Jewish tradition about 1520, either as a result of the immigration of the Spanish exiles or in the wake of the Turkish conquest of 1518. Thenceforth all literary sources describe it as a place of assembly and prayer for Jews. According to a tradition transmitted by Moses Ḥagiz[26], it was the sultan Selim the conqueror of Jerusalem who recovered the Wall from underneath the dungheap which was hiding it and granted permission to the Jews to hold prayers there. No Muslim sources about Jerusalem bear any evidence of Arab interest in the Western Wall. The nearby area became Muslim religious property at the end of the 12th century, and from 1320 there

[22] Jewish traveler (second half of 12th cent.)
[23] First topographer of Ereẓ Israel (1280–1355?)
[24] Italian traveler (15th century)
[25] Italian rabbi and Mishnah commentator (c. 1450–before 1516)
[26] Scholar, kabbalist and opponent of Shabbateanism (1672–1751)

כותל המערבי

The Western Wall on the seal (reversed) of the Jerusalem community, 16th–17th century. Tel Aviv, I. Einhorn Collection.
Photo David Harris, Jerusalem.

is mention of the Moghrabi Quarter established there.
Nevertheless, Jews were able to hold their prayers at the
Wall undisturbed.

With the expansion of the Jewish population in Ereẓ
Israel from the beginning of the 19th century onward, and
with the increase in visitors, the popularity of the Western
Wall grew among Jews. Its image began to appear in Jewish
folkloristic art (upon ritual articles, seals, and title pages)
and later also in modern art drawings (B. Shatz, J.
Steinhardt, M. Chagall, and others). It also became a
164 subject of literary creation. The 19th century also saw the

beginning of the archaeological study of the Western Wall north and south of the open prayer spot. In 1838 Robinson[27] discovered the arch since named after him, and in the 1850s Barclay[28] laid bare the ancient gate (now in the corner of the women's section). In 1865 Wilson[29] described the bridge discovered by Tobler in the 1830s. In 1867 Sir Charles Warren[30] sank shafts to reveal the full height of the wall.

During the 19th century attempts were made on behalf of the Jewish community in connection with the Wall. In the 1850s Ḥakham Abdullah of Bombay failed in his efforts to buy the Wall. Sir Moses Montefiore[31] tried in vain to obtain permission for placing benches or for installing a protection against rain there. Permission to pave the street was, however, granted. Occasionally a table for the reading of the Torah was placed near the Wall, but had to be soon removed at the demands of the Muslim religious authorities. In 1887 Baron Rothschild[32] offered to buy the whole Moghrabi Quarter, and have it demolished. He proposed to the government that for the funds received the Waqf should obtain other lands and resettle there the residents evacuated from the Moghrabi Quarter. Although negotiations had reached an advanced stage the plan never materialized for reasons not properly clarified to the present day. It is probable that objections were raised not only on the part of the Waqf, but also on the part of the rabbis and communal leaders of the Sephardi community on whose full cooperation Rothschild made conditional his handling of this delicate matter. It appears that certain rabbis observed that the conditions laid down for the designated Jewish sacred trust (hekdesh) would convert the area into a public domain (reshut ha-rabbim) with regard to carrying on the

[27] U.S. orientalist (1794–1863)
[28] American missionary (19th cent.)
[29] British army officer and topographer (1836–1905)
[30] British army officer and archaeologist (1840–1927)
[31] British Jewish leader and philanthropist (1784–1885)
[32] Philanthropist, patron of Jewish settlement in Erez Israel (1845–1934)

"Jews at the Wailing Wall," drawing by Leonid Pasternak. London, Lydia Pasternak Slater Collection.

Sabbath and thus create halakhic difficulties. In addition interests and counter-interests among the trustees of the various Sephardi sacred trusts foiled the plan.

Shortly before World War I, a further attempt to purchase the surroundings of the Western Wall was made by 166 the Anglo-Palestine Bank. These negotiations were interrupted by the outbreak of the war. In 1912 the Turkish authorities ordered the removal of a partition between men and women, benches, a glass cupboard for candles, a table for reading the Torah, etc. about the introduction of which the Waqf had complained.

After the Balfour Declaration and the British Mandate had given the Jews a recognized national status in Erez Israel, they began to add national significance to the traditional religious significance of the Western Wall. The Arab mufti incited his community against the Zionists (who, he claimed, intended to seize control of the Wall) by proclaiming it a sacred Muslim site which he named after the legendary horse "Al-Burak," upon which Mohammed is supposed to have ridden to Jerusalem and which he allegedly tied to this wall during his visit. Many intercommunal conflicts about the Western Wall occurred in the 1920s. In order to antagonize the Jews the mufti ordered the opening of a gate at the southern end of the street thus converting it into a thoroughfare for passersby and animals. In addition the Muslims deliberately held loud-voiced ceremonies in the vicinity. They also complained again about the placing of accessories of worship near the Wall, and a partition (between men and women) was forcibly removed—by the British police—on the Day of Atonement 1928. In August 1929 an instigated Muslim crowd rioted among the worshipers and destroyed ritual objects and, following the excitement and unrest this created, murderous riots broke out a few days later.

The British set up a committee of inquiry and consequently an international committee (consisting of a Swede, a Swiss, and a Dutchman) was appointed by the League of Nations to resolve "the problem of the Wall." It conducted in Jerusalem, in the summer of 1930, "the trial of the Wall." It came to three main conclusions: (a) the Muslims had absolute ownership of the Wall; (b) the Jews had the uncontested right to worship and to place seats in the street; (c) the Jews were not to blow the *shofar* there. The Arabs objected. The Jews accepted, except for the prohibition to blow the *shofar* which was considered a searing humiliation. 167

The Western Wall, on the first anniversary of the reunification of Jerusalem, 1968. Photo Werner Braun, Jerusalem.

Indeed, each year nationalist youths would blow the *shofar* near the Wall at the termination of the Day of Atonement, which would always lead to the intervention of the British police.

From December 1947, after bloody incidents with the Arabs, Jews were no longer able to approach the Western Wall and after the capitulation of the Jewish Quarter (of the Old City) in May 1948, Jews were prevented for 19 years from even looking at the Wall from afar. The paragraph in the cease-fire agreement granting freedom of access to the holy places was not kept by the Jordanians.

The Wall was liberated on the third day of the Six-Day **168** War (June 7, 1967) by Israel's parachutists breaking through the "bloody gate," which the mufti had opened. The Moghrabi Quarter was immediately demolished and on the first day of Shavuot, one-quarter of a million Jews swarmed to the place. Subsequently the buildings placed against the Wall in its continuation southward were removed. The entire cleared area in front of the Western Wall was leveled and converted into a large paved open space. The lower square near the Wall is the prayer area, where one may find people praying or studying, either singly or in groups, day and night throughout the year. The excavations made by Warren in 1867, north of the Wall beneath the Muslim structures, have been renewed and extended. They have already uncovered the continuation of the Wall northward beyond Wilson's bridge. To the south, too, archaeological excavations are being conducted and the fully impressive extent of the Wall is being progressively revealed.

6 THE HOLY SEPULCHER

The present Church of the Holy Sepulcher in Jerusalem houses the traditional sites of the Crucifixion (Golgotha), the burial place and Resurrection of Jesus, and is one of the most sacred spots in the world to Christianity. Within the church are found the last five stations, out of the fourteen, of the Via Dolorosa. The present location of the church has been disputed because it lies within the city walls, whereas the Crucifixion was outside. But Christianity in general accepts the present location holding that the ancient city wall ran to the south of the present church; in addition they maintain that the Jewish sepulcher chamber, located in the section reserved for the Syrian Jacobites (St. Nicodemus) in the west of the church, is the sepulcher of Joseph of Arimathea in which the body of Jesus was laid (Matthew 27:57–60). Some have doubted the authenticity of the traditional sites of the Holy Sepulcher and Golgotha (Calvary). In 1883 General Charles George Gordon (1833–1885), known as Gordon of Khartoum, identified a group of rock-hewn tombs of the Second Temple period behind a skull-shaped rock, outside the present city walls in the north, as Golgotha where the Crucifixion occurred, and this is known at present as the Garden Tomb and as Protestant Golgotha.

The present church is a conglomeration of three periods of construction dating from the Byzantine Era, the Crusader Period and the 19th century. In 326 Helena, the mother of Constantine the Great, while on a pilgrimage to the Holy Land, found what she claimed to be the Holy Cross

The Church of the Holy Sepulcher in Jerusalem.
Courtesy Ministry of Tourism. Photo A. Strajmayster, Jerusalem.

in a disused cistern at the present site of the Holy Sepulcher. In 335 by order of Constantine an outstanding Church was built there. The entrance was from the east through a Roman colonnaded road into an open court surrounded by porticos, and at the end of which stood the basilica proper, later called *Martyrium* (place of witnessing) dedicated to the Holy Cross. Beyond the basilica was a second open court where the rock of Calvary stood. Behind this court was the Sepulchral Cavern, enclosed by a round domed building which became known as the Anastasis. Only a few fragmentary portions of these Constantinian structures remain today.

In 614 the Persians burned the Constantinian building. Restoration work was carried out soon after but on a   171 reduced and less lavish plan, and the Church continued in use under the Arabs after 637. In 1010 the Egyptian Caliph al-Ḥākim ordered the demolition of the Holy Sepulcher so that very little remained. Ḥākim's successors showed more tolerance and in the mid-11th century the main structures of the Holy Sepulcher were rebuilt.

The Crusaders upon their conquest of the city in 1099 proceeded to unite all the sanctuaries in one building. The Rotunda or Anastasis, was for the most part preserved, the Sepulcher repaired and encased in a new edicule (a little shrine), and a new Romanesque church was erected facing the Rotunda. A long period of tranquillity lasted until 1808 when a fire caused considerable damage to the Sepulcher. Repairs were made and a new edicule was designated in a Russian style. Further repairs have been made up to the present time.

The church is entered by a single portal. Within the entrance is the stone of Unction which marks the place where Jesus was anointed before burial. Nearby, to the left, is the Rotunda, in which stands the edicule of the Holy Sepulcher directly under an iron dome supported by eighteen pillars. The edicule has two chambers, the Chapel of the Angel and the Sepulcher proper, the 14th station of the Cross. Behind the edicule is the chapel of the Copts and opposite is the Chapel of St. Nicodemus where the Sepulcher of Joseph of Arimathea is located. On the east side of the Rotunda is the Katholikon (Orthodox Cathedral) with a stone in it that marks "the center of the world". On the right side of the entrance is a stairway to Calvary, the Rock of Golgotha, $14\frac{1}{2}$ feet (5 m.) above ground level, divided into two chapels. The southern chapel is the Latin Calvary the scene of the 10th and 11th stations of the Cross, the other chapel is the Greek Calvary the scene of the 12th station. Between the two chapels is the altar of the Stabat Mater, the 13th station. Behind the Katholikon is the Church of St. Helena to which one descends by a flight of stairs. From this chapel another flight of stairs leads to 172 the Chapel of the Finding of the Holy Cross.

The Holy Sepulcher is controlled in practice largely by the Greek Orthodox, Latin, and Armenian patriarchates. The Syrians and the Copts have small chapels within its precincts, while the Ethiopians and Anglicans have the use of chapels in its immediate vicinity. This situation is the "provisional" result of centuries of struggle between the various churches over the holy places (see above). Since the question of the holy places has never been solved, the position has been left, by agreement, in *status quo ante*. Two Moslem families hold by hereditary right, from the time of Saladin, the offices of custodian of the keys and the opening of the doors of the Church.

7 ḤARAM AL-SHARIF

Ḥaram al-Sharif (in Arabic "The Noble Sanctuary") is a complex of buildings situated on the Temple Mount, traditionally identified as Mount Moriah, in Jerusalem, and is the third most sacred place to Muslims, after Mecca and Medina. It is a trapezoid-shaped (approximately rectangular) walled-in area of approximately 35 acres (140 dunams). The four walls surrounding it (the western one is the Western Wall, see above), date—at least in their lower parts—from the time of Herod's Temple (end of 1st century B.C.E.). The entire enclosure consists of an esplanade or courtyard, surrounding an elevated platform (4 m. (13 ft.) higher) occupying approximately $5\frac{1}{2}$ acres (23 dunams) surrounded by arched structures. Part of the esplanade is "artificial" being the massive *Millo* ("fill") executed by Solomon and Herod to enlarge the platform for the purpose of the Temple-building. In each of the walls there are a number of gates, those in the eastern and southern walls are from the Second Temple era, and are blocked, and those in the northern and western walls date from the Arab conquest time (638) onward and are still in service.

Within the area of Ḥaram al-Sharif there are about 100 different structures from various periods, among them great works of art and craftsmanship, including open Muslim prayer spots (some of them with small domes), arched porticos, Madrasas (Muslim religious schools), minarets, and fountains (some for drinking and others for worshipers to wash their hands and feet before prayer).

Underneath the present-day "artificial" surface of the

mount there are 34 cisterns. There are also substructures—
the ancient Al-Aqsa and the largest which is known as
"Solomon's stables". Two of the buildings on the site the
Qubat al-Sakhra (Arab. Dome of the Rock wrongly called
"Mosque of Omar") and the Al-Aqsa Mosque are of
especial religious significance for the Muslims.

Qubat al-Sakhra (Dome of the Rock). In 684 C.E. the
Ummayyad caliph Abd al-Malik began this building and
it was completed seven years later. The building was not
intended to serve as a mosque, but only as a shrine or as a
glorious dome over the Sacred Rock, located approximately
in the middle of the elevated platform, and from this it
derives its name. This also explains the design of the
building that has nothing in common with the regular
plan of a mosque. The building is a regular octagon,
each side 63 feet (21 m.) and its diameter 180 feet (60 m.).
The dome rises from a cylindrical drum to a height of
108 feet (36 m.) above ground. The rock under the Dome is
identified by the Muslims as the great altar of holocausts
and the cave under the rock as the place where ashes and
other sacrificial refuse were collected. They also identify
it with the *even shetiyyah* i.e., the rock that was inside the
Holy of Holies, and from the same rock, according to
Muslim tradition, Muhammad ascended to heaven (*miraj*).
The Dome of the Rock is considered as one of the most
beautiful works of Islamic architecture.

Al-Aqsa. Near the southern wall of the Temple Mount
stands the Al-Aqsa Mosque built by Abd al-Malik in
about 700 C.E. on the spot where Caliph Omar in 638 is
supposed to have offered his prayers (according to some
historians it was completed in 709–15 by his son Caliph al-
Walid). The name, Al-Aqsa, meaning "furthermost" (from
Mecca) as mentioned in the Koran (Sura 17:2) in the
description of the prophet's miraculous journey from Mecca
(*isra*).The Al-Aqsa is built in the form of a Byzantine basilica,
but its Ummayyad origin is clear. It has often been
destroyed by earthquakes and other disasters. The present
building was constructed in 1033 C.E. The eastern wing of 175

Al-Aqṣa is the Mosque of Omar. There exists a custom among the Muslims to circuit the Al-Aqṣa in an opposite direction to the circuit of the Ka'ba, the Black Stone of Mecca.

After the conquest of Jerusalem by the Crusaders (1099), the Dome of the Rock was converted into a church and called Templum Domini (the Temple of the Lord) and Al-Aqṣa became a church called Templum Solomonis (Solomon's Temple). They were converted into Muslim houses of prayer after Saladin's conquest of Jerusalem in 1187 and have remained so ever since.

The Temple Mount, with the Dome of the Rock in the center and the Al-Aqṣā Mosque in the foreground. Photo Werner Braun, Jerusalem.

Part Five:

PILGRIMAGE

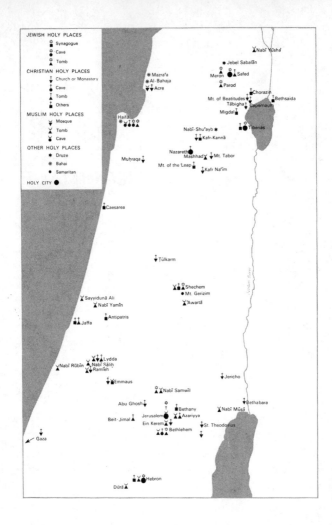

JEWISH HOLY PLACES
- ⌂ Synagogue
- ⌂ Cave
- ⌂ Tomb

CHRISTIAN HOLY PLACES
- ✝ Church or Monastery
- ✝ Cave
- ✝ Tomb
- ✝ Others

MUSLIM HOLY PLACES
- ⩔ Mosque
- ⩔ Tomb
- ▲ Cave

OTHER HOLY PLACES
- ✳ Druze
- ✳ Bahai
- ● Samaritan

HOLY CITY ●

Nabī Yūshaʿ
Jebel Sabalān
Meron Safed
Parod
Chorazin Bethsaida
Mt. of Beatitudes Tābigha Capernaum
Migdal
Mazraʿa
Al-Bahaja
Acre
Haifa
Nabī-Shuʿayb
Kafr-Kannā
Tiberias
Nazareth
Mashhad Mt. Tabor
Muhraqa
Mt. of the Leap Kafr Naʿim

Caesarea

Tülkarm

Shechem
Mt. Gerizim
ʿAwartā
Sayyidunā Ali
Nabī Yamīn
Antipatris
Jaffa

Nabī Rūbīn
Lydda
Nabī Sālih
Ramleh
Emmaus
Nabī Samwīl
Abu Ghosh
Jericho
Bethany
Jerusalem ʿAzariyya
Nabī Mūsā Bethabara
Beit-Jimal
Ein Kerem
Bethlehem St. Theodosius
Gaza

Hebron
Dūrā

178 Main centers of religious pilgrimage in Israel.

PILGRIMAGE

In Hebrew the term *aliyah* (lit. "going up") has been used since ancient times for pilgrimages to Jerusalem on the three festivals known as *shalosh regalim*. The Torah prescribes that all males must go up to Jerusalem "three times a year" on the three festivals—Passover, Shavuot, and Sukkot (Ex. 23:17; 34:23; Deut. 16:16; II Chron. 8:13).

Second Temple Period. Hundreds of thousands of pilgrims from within Ereẓ Israel as well as from the Diaspora streamed to the Temple at each of the three festivals. The pilgrimage affected the life of every Jew, who might have to prepare for the occasion, and the journey and the accompanying sacrifices involved a not inconsiderable financial outlay. The inspiration derived from "the sojourn in the Temple courts," and from attendance at the rabbinical academies in Jerusalem, remained a powerful stimulus to the pilgrim after his return: "His heart prompts him to study Torah" (TJ, Suk. 5:1, 55a). Many of the new trends in Jewish spiritual life were ventilated in Jerusalem, and the pilgrim served as the vehicle for disseminating the ideas that were in constant ferment during the period. The pilgrimage had a considerable influence upon the life of the capital in a number of spheres; in the social sphere, from the presence there of Jews from every part of the Diaspora, and in the economic, from the vast sums spent by the thousands of pilgrims both for their own needs and on charity. It also had a national-political influence. The *aliyah* from all parts of Ereẓ Israel and the Diaspora strengthened the consciousness of national and social solidarity (Jos., Ant. 4:203-4). This national consciousness reached a new peak with the presence of the throngs of pilgrims in Jerusalem and made them even more sensitive to the humiliation entailed in their subjection to a foreign yoke. As a result of this sensitivity, disorders and revolts were of frequent occurrence in Jerusalem during the festivals (Jos., Wars 5:243-4; Ant. 13:337-9).

The biblical injunction on the subject states: "Three times in the year shall all thy males appear before the Lord God" (Ex. 23:17; 34:23, Deut. 16:16). These passages were apparently not construed as mandatory, requiring *aliyah* thrice yearly, but as meaning that on these occasions it was a meritorious act to make the pilgrimage and in so doing offer up sacrifices, "and none shall appear before me empty" *(ibid.)*. The tannaitic sources speak of the obligation of *aliyah le-regel* but not of a commandment to go up on every festival (Ḥag. 1:1, 6a). In any event it is clear that not all the male population of Ereẓ Israel, and certainly not of the Diaspora, made the pilgrimage three times yearly. Although both from the Talmud (Pes. 8b) and from Josephus (Wars 2:515) one might infer that the whole population of a city would participate in the pilgrimage, it was not general that the cities, even those near to Jerusalem, would be entirely emptied as a consequence of their Jewish population going on pilgrimage. On the other hand, there can be no doubt that a considerable number went up, especially from Judea (Wars 2:43). There is ample evidence of *aliyah le-regel* from Galilee, and it may be assumed that the number who came from the Diaspora was not as great as those from Ereẓ Israel. Philo mentions that "countless multitudes from countless cities come to the Temple at every festival, some by land, and others by sea, from east and west and north and south" (Spec. 1:69). Sources in the Talmud, Josephus, and the New Testament yield a long list of places, including Babylonia, Persia, Media, Alexandria, Cyrenaica, Ethiopia, Syria, Pontus, Asia, Tarsus, Phrygia, Pamphylia, and Rome, whose residents were to be found in

Jerusalem during the festivals (ARN², 27, 55; Meg. 26a; Jos., Ant. 17:26; Acts 2:9–10). Both the inscription of Theodotus found in Jerusalem and the literary sources indicate that sometimes the inhabitants of a particular city would establish synagogues in Jerusalem and hospices for the pilgrims who required such facilites (Tosef., Meg. 3:6; Acts 6:9; M. Schwabe, in *Sefer Yerushalayim,* ed. by M. Avi-Yonah, 1 (1956), 362).

The Pilgrimage. The pilgrims often traveled in caravans which mustered in the cities of Erez Israel and the Diaspora. The ascent of the joyful throng of celebrants to Jerusalem is already mentioned in a number of Psalms such as Psalms 42, 84, and 122, which are songs of the pilgrim companies, and it is reflected in many rabbinic passages (cf. Lam. R. 1:17, no. 52). The procession on the occasion of the first fruits of Shavuot was particularly impresssive: "Those who lived near brought fresh figs and grapes, but those from a distance brought dried figs and raisins. An ox with horns bedecked with gold and with an olive crown on its head led the way. The flute was played before them until they were near Jerusalem" (Bik. 3:3). Josephus relates that the pilgrims from Babylonia used to assemble in Nehardea and Nisibis and accompany the convoys transporting the annual half-*shekel* Temple dues on the journey to Jerusalem (Ant. 18:311–2). Women also took part, the biblical passage "all thy males shall appear" being understood merely as referring only to the duty of the men who alone were obliged to bring the obligatory sacrifices (Ant. 11:109; Luke 2:41–43).

The Rituals. The pilgrims arrived in Jerusalem several days before the festival; this was especially true of those from the Diaspora who had to undergo purification for over a week from the defilement incurred in alien lands (Jos., Wars 1:229; 6:290). The essence of the pilgrimage was the entry of the individual, or the group, into the Temple to worship there on the festivals, and the offering of the obligatory sacrifices enjoined in the precept that, "None shall appear before me empty." The tannaitic tradition 181 expounded that the celebrant was obliged to offer the pilgrim's burnt offering, the festal offering which is counted as a peace offering, and the offering of rejoicing (Hag. 6b). The sacrifices were offered both on the first day or during subsequent days of the festival.

The Stay in Jerusalem. According to the *halakhah*, not only did the scriptural verse, "and in the morning you shall turn and go to your tent," enjoined with regard to the Passover pilgrim, oblige him to remain overnight in Jerusalem, but "in the morning" was interpreted as the morning after the last day of the festival. The pilgrim was thus obliged to stop over for the entire Passover week, and for the eight days of Sukkot (Zev. 11:7 and 97a; Tosef. Hag. 1:5). The celebrants used to stay in the capital itself, or in the adjoining villages, or encamp in tents erected in the surrounding fields (Jos., Ant. 17:217; Wars 2:12). During their sojourn in Jerusalem the pilgrims engaged in study of the Torah and participated in the common festive meals at which they ate the permitted sacrificial food—the peace offering, as well as the second tithe which had to be consumed in Jerusalem (Jos., Ant. 4:205). Greater leniency was applied to the law appertaining to ritual defilement during the festival, in order that the laws of ritual purity would not prevent social intercourse. Jerusalem was regarded as the common possession of the entire Jewish people, and householders in the capital were forbidden to take rent from the pilgrims, who however left them the hides of the sacrificial animals as a token of gratitude (Tosef., Ma'as Sh. 1:12 and 13; ARN[1] 35, 103). The sources indicate that a convivial atmosphere prevailed in the capital during the days of pilgrimages: "Nobody ever had occasion to say to his neighbor 'I have been unable to find a stove for cooking the paschal meals in Jerusalem,' or 'I have been unable to find a bed to sleep in Jerusalem'" (ARN *ibid.*).

Post-Temple Period. Pilgrimages to Jerusalem continued after the destruction of the Temple (cf. Ned. 23a). However, the joy that previously characterized these events was now combined with sorrow. When the pilgrims encountered the site of the ruined Sanctuary they rended their garments as a sign of mourning and recited the verse, "Our holy and our beautiful house, where our fathers praised Thee, is burned with fire and all our pleasant things are laid waste" (Isa. 64:10; MK 26a). Some even abstained from meat and wine on the day they saw Jerusalem in its destruction (Shevu. 20a). The rabbis, commenting on the verse, "These things I remember, and pour out my soul within me" (Ps. 52:5), compared the pilgrimages before and after the destruction. Previously, the Jews went up to Jerusalem along well-kept roads, the trees forming a covering over their heads, and under the protection of a government committed to God. Now they went through thorny hedges, exposed to the sun, and under the sovereignty of oppressive governments (Lam. R. 1:52). Nevertheless, the Jews continued their pilgrimages to the Temple site, and in 333 "the traveler of Bordeaux" described Jews pouring oil on a stone. In 392 Jerome related that Jews came to lament the destruction of the Temple, after paying for a permit to enter the Temple grounds (commentary on Zeph. 1:16). A fifth-century testimony reported a pilgrimage of over 100,000 Jews, made possible as a result of the sympathetic attitude of Anthenais Eudocia, wife of the emperor Theodosius II.

These pilgrimages continued throughout the Middle Ages although on many occasions the Jewish pilgrims were subject to taxes and discriminatory regulations which were enacted against them by the Christian or Muslim overlords of the holy places. The ninth-century pilgrimages of Rabbi Ahimaaz the Elder, of Venosa, Italy, are well known. The Persian traveler Nāsir Khosraw (1047) stated that he saw Jews from Roman lands (Byzantium) coming to visit their houses of worship. The testimony of a pilgrim from Babylonia, Phinehas ha-Kohen (c. 1030), has also survived.

After Erez Israel was conquered by the Muslims under Saladin (1187), the Jews were once again permitted to visit their holy places freely. Numerous pilgrims came from Damascus, Babylonia, and Egypt, and they remained in Jerusalem over Passover and Shavuot. Naḥmanides, in a letter to his son, wrote: "Many men and women from Damascus, Babylon, and their vicinities come to Jerusalem to see the site of the Holy Temple and to lament its destruction." The commandment of pilgrimage was also a factor in motivating the journeys of Benjamin of Tudela and Pethahiah of Regensburg in the 12th century, and Jacob b. Nethanel and Judah al-Ḥarizi in the 13th. In his writing, Benjamin referred to the Dome of the Rock, standing "opposite the place of the holy Temple which is occupied at present by [a church called] Templum Domini . . . In front of it you see the Western Wall, one of the walls which formed the ancient Temple . . . and all Jews go there to say their prayers near the wall of the courtyard."

The number of pilgrims was greatly increased by the many exiles who settled in Turkish territory following the 1492 expulsion of the Jews from Spain. The tomb of Samuel the Prophet at Nabi Samwil (thought to be the biblical Ramah) was also a goal of their pilgrimages. Here they held annual celebrations similar to those which were instituted in Meron on Lag Ba-Omer, a century later. In 1634, Gershom ben Eliezer Ha-Levi of Prague visited the Holy Land, and later recorded his experience in *Gelilot Erez Yisrael* (Prague, 1824⁴). The most famous pilgrimage made to the Holy Land by early ḥasidic leaders was that of Naḥman of Bratslav. His visit (1798–99) left such a profound impression upon him that when he later returned to Poland, he remarked, "Wherever I go, I am still in Erez Israel."

In modern times, the pilgrimages most beneficial to the Holy Land were those of Sir Moses Montefiore. He made his first visit in 1827, and returned in 1838, 1849, 1855, 1866, and 1875. He made his last pilgrimage when he was 91 years old, and after each visit he intensified his financial support for the new *yishuv*. With the continuing development of the Jewish resettlement in Erez Israel and the improvement in the means of long-distance transportation, Jews continued in ever-increasing numbers to visit the Holy Land.

With the conclusion of the armistice agreement following the Israel War of Independence (1949), it was agreed between Jordan and Israel that talks would follow immediately to enable "free access to the holy places" in Jerusalem, and the "use of the Jewish cemetery on the Mount of Olives." However, nothing ever came of this and Jerusalem remained a divided city. This caused difficulties for pilgrims who desired to visit the shrines in both countries. While Jordan finally did make some arrangements for Christian pilgrims to enter or leave through one of the crossing points (the main one being the Mandelbaum Gate in Jerusalem), Jewish pilgrims were not allowed into Jordan at all. Most distressing to Jews was the denial of access to the Western Wall. The main goal of the pilgrims then became the traditional Tomb of David on Mount Zion from where they viewed the Old City of Jerusalem. Following the Six-Day War and the reunification of Jerusalem, the Western Wall was again reopened to Jews and became a magnet of pilgrimage.

Christian Pilgrimages. Christian pilgrimages to Erez Israel became an established institution from the fourth century on, and have continued almost uninterruptedly to the present day. The reports of the pilgrims had a wide influence, stimulating religious piety and curiosity about the Holy Land. They also provide an important source of information for the history of Erez Israel, the political situation in various periods, its communities, sects, settlements, and social life. Despite its anti-Jewish bias, the pilgrim literature also gives a general picture of Jewish settlement in Erez Israel, supplementing and augmenting the Jewish sources in many details.

HISTORY. Erez Israel became the Holy Land to Christians as the cradle of Christianity and because of its associations with the life of Jesus and the apostles. Nevertheless the Church never aspired to make Jerusalem the center of Christianity, and its symbolic significance was in its mystic-heavenly sense (see Gal. 4:24–26 and Rev. 21). The primacy of the mystical, heavenly Jerusalem in

Christian thought on the one hand, and the concrete association of the Holy Land with the life and death of Jesus on the other, resulted in an ambivalent attitude to pilgrimages by some of the Christian writers. While popular piety and devotion naturally tended toward a veneration of the holy places, many writers warned against the danger of a "carnal" and material misunderstanding of essentially spiritual realities. In fact, many early Church Fathers at first discouraged pilgrimage. Jerome declared that the gates of heaven were open to believers equally in Britain as Jerusalem (Ep. 58 *Ad Paulinum*). He mentions that St. Hilarion, who lived in the Holy Land for 50 years, prided himself on the fact that he had visited the holy places only once. However the ardent wish of Christians to visit the Holy Land was eventually accepted by Jerome, who settled in a cave near Bethlehem. In practice pilgrimage was first stimulated under Constantine (306–337), with the announcement by his mother Helena of the discovery of the cross in Jerusalem, and the erection by Constantine of the magnificent rotunda and basilica at the presumed sepulcher of Jesus. Christians thereupon readily identified other places mentioned in the New Testament associated with Jesus and the apostles. The sites were immediately sanctified, and shrines or churches built near them (cf. E. Robinson, *Biblical Researches in Palestine* (1841), 371).

These attracted an increasing stream of pilgrims, interrupted only by political insecurity or pestilence, and reaching huge proportions in the Middle Ages. The Crusades were preeminently a pilgrimage of armies, aimed at liberating the holy places from the Muslims, whatever their accompanying political motives. The duty of caring for the protection and needs of pilgrims gave rise to the influential hospitaller orders, such as the Knights Templar and the Knights of Malta. In the later Middle Ages the religious factor diminished to be replaced increasingly by commerical motives. Even in the ninth and tenth centuries the Muslim rulers had encouraged trade there, and Jerusalem became a large entrepôt between East and West.

One result of the trading contacts between Europe and the East was the extension of the maritime power of the Italian republics, especially Venice and Genoa, during the Fourth Crusade (1202–04).

CHARACTER OF THE PILGRIMAGES. Jerusalem and Bethlehem remained the main centers of Christian pilgrimage, but there were others, especially in Galilee. However places in Galilee such as Nazareth, Capernaum, Magdala, or Kefar Kanna are not mentioned by early pilgrims, such as the Bordeaux pilgrim whose *Itinerarium Burdigalense* (written before 333) is the first pilgrim guide extant. This was probably because Galilee then still had a mainly Jewish population.

The chief incentive to pilgrimage remained religious. Pilgrimages were organized to gain remission of sins, as set penances, in fulfillment of vows, for atonements for crimes, for cures, and for the acquisition of relics. However they also fulfilled other purposes: the desire to see foreign lands, people and customs, love of adventure, and commercial profit. Thus, besides the thousands of the pious, the pilgrim movement attracted a bevy of adventurers, sick persons, and paupers. The journey of the pilgrim was fraught with danger. He faced local wars, attack by pirates or brigands, epidemics, bad sanitation, or arbitrary imprisonment by the local authority. In Venice in the 15th century he was given facilities to make his will before embarking. The departure of a pilgrim also posed a problem for the Church. It meant disruption of family life and the absence of a breadwinner or worker, while the conditions of the journey frequently brought a lowering of moral standards. The Church therefore insisted that pilgrims should obtain written authorizations from the bishop or abbot for their journey. If he met the Church's requirements the pilgrim received its blessing and assistance.

THE LITERATURE. Once home the pilgrim reported the glories of the holy places and the wonders he had seen and heard. These accounts circulated both by word of mouth and in written records or itineraries for the guidance of

Pilgrims making their way to Jerusalem. An engraving
of 1581 reproduced in S. Schweigger, *Reyssbeschreibung aus
Teutschland nach Jerusalem,* 1608.

future pilgrims. Although until the end of the Middle Ages
the oral accounts were predominant as the vast majority of
pilgrims were uneducated, a growing number of travelers
recorded their journey and impressions. Roehricht's bibliography of Palestiniana in the main European languages
lists 38 authors between the years 333 and 1000, 517 up to
the year 1500, and nearly 2,000 between the years 1800 and
1878. Subsequently there has been an inordinate increase
of such records.

The record usually followed a set scheme providing a
description of the Holy Land and the spiritual experiences
of the pilgrims for those who had never been there. From
the end of the 17th century much was written for the
purposes of religious propaganda. The authors frequently
catered to their audience and supplemented their descriptions with embellishments and imaginary adventures, where
reality and legend intermingle. However, many present an
188   accurate if limited record, often closely resembling one

Page from a 16th-century Hebrew "pilgrims' guide," with a description of the Mt. of Olives and pictorial representations of the house of Huldah, the Pillar of Absalom, and the grave of Zechariah. *Casale Pilgrim,* fol. 4v, Casale Monferrato, Italy, 1598. Cecil Roth Collection. Photo Werner Braun, Jerusalem.

another. The records fall into several different categories. Some are on-the-spot accounts of events as they occurred. Many were written down after the pilgrim's return, often on the basis of notes taken on the journey, which contained details omitted from his book. A large number were written on the basis of previous works, including many passages merely copied from them or with deliberate variations. The German cleric Ludolf von Suchem (1336–41) states that he did not see all that he wrote with his own eyes, but drew on ancient history books. *The Travels of Sir John Mandeville* (in the Holy Land, 1336) is a collection of earlier sources. Some writers quote their sources, and some copy them without acknowledgment. A number, especially in the early period, related their accounts to a third person who recorded them in turn. The account of the French bishop Arculfus (670) was recorded by an abbot in Iona, off Scotland.

Educated pilgrims and scholars later made independent **189** investigations instead of accepting everything they were told. Many, who reveal wide learning, relate the old traditions but with reservations. Fynes Moryson (16th century), although criticizing the credibility of the tales told by the monks of the Latin monastery, was still deeply impressed and moved by what he saw. The pioneer of modern researches was the U.S. theologian, philologist, and geographer Edward Robinson (1837) who voiced a much stronger and well-founded criticism of the credulity accorded by the pilgrims down the ages who had always seen the holy places through the eyes of their monastic cicerones. He considered that many sites had no historical basis and even contradicted the evidence of the New Testament. He also cast doubt on the traditions associated with Eusebius and Jerome, from which others had originated. Robinson therefore carried out his pioneer researches independently of the Christian orders in Erez Israel.

Information on the Jews. Much of the information available on Jewish life in the Holy Land in earlier periods comes from the Christian pilgrim accounts. Thus, Jacobus de Verona (1335), an Augustinian friar, speaks of Jewish guides. Ludolf von Suchem states that Jews, but not Christians, were allowed on payment to enter the cave of Machpelah in Hebron, where the Patriarchs are buried. An anonymous Englishman (1345) tells of Jews living in caves near Jerusalem. Arnold von Harff, a German nobleman from Erft, though as prejudiced against the Jews as most of the early pilgrims, showed a more intelligent interest in them. Among "the very many" Jews in Jerusalem, with some of whom he entered into learned discussion, he found several natives of Lombardy knowledgeable about Christianity, three from Germany, and also two monks who had converted to Judaism. He learned some Hebrew and his book reproduces the *alef-bet* and also a number of words and phrases in common use, from his transliterations of which it is clear that he learned them from people of Central European origin. Pierre Belon (1547), a French physician of Mans, saw in Galilee Jews engaged in fishing; and newly established villages, where, he notes, they were converting wasteland into fertile areas.

Much is reported about Safed as a flourishing Jewish center. A Franciscan from Spain (1553–55), whose name is not known, found a Jewish population of 8,000–10,000 there. William Biddulph (1600), an English priest, mentions the Hebrew that was taught there (as well as in Salonika).

John Sanderson (1601), an English merchant, traveled with a Jewish merchant who hid his money in his clothes, some 12,000 ducats, of which 3,000 was for charity and for books in the Holy Land. The Franciscan Eugenius Roger (1629–34), who estimates 15,000 Jews in the country, including 4,000 in Jerusalem, divides them into two groups: the old-established oriental Jews and the newcomers from Europe, particularly Spain, Germany, and Italy. There was little intermarriage between the two groups, the first being particularly doubtful of the authenticity of the Jewishness of those from Spain, "for they had been baptized, had for long lived as Christians and ate foods and drank drinks forbidden by the Law of Moses." Other communal troubles are reported by the Jesuit Michael Nau, who visited the land in 1665 and again in 1674. He found the Jews divided into the Rabbanites, who accepted the Talmud, and the Karaites and the Samaritans, who accepted only the Bible. Each complained to him about the other: "They hate one another with an unparalleled hatred. But there is one thing about which they must agree in Jerusalem, that is, that they must pay heavily to the Turks for the right to remain there."

A vivid description of the unhappy condition of the Jews in Jerusalem is given by Chateaubriand[33] (1806–07): "isolated from the other inhabitants, abandoned to every kind of shame . . ., he suffers every humiliation without crying out against it, without a sound turns his cheek to him who strikes him," and Chateaubriand adds sympathetically that

[33] French writer (1768–1848)

there is nothing more remarkable in the history of the nations than the survival of the Jews—a miracle "even in the eyes of a *philosophe*."

Another sympathetic observer is Alphonse de Lamartine[34] (1832–33) who writes: "This land, if settled by a new Jewish people . . . is destined once again to become the Promised Land . . . if He who watches from above will return the people to it and give them the political privileges of peace and security." Robert Curzon[35] (1834) states: "It is noteworthy that the Jews who are born in Jerusalem are completely different from those we see in Europe. Here they are of a blond race, light in movement, and, especially, refined in their conduct." At the same time John Lloyd Stephens[36] (1835) tells of the fear under which the Jews lived in Hebron and Safed.

Edward Robinson remarks about Christian missionary activity among the Jews: "So far the efforts of the English mission have had only the most meager success." He also describes the devastation wrought by the great earthquake of 1837. Another visitor was William Bartlett[37] (1842 and 1853) who gave exact descriptions of Jerusalem.

William Holt Yates (1843), London physician and orientalist, exemplifies an attitude toward the country radically different from the pilgrims of the earlier centuries. He thinks that Palestine (and Asia Minor and Syria) would benefit by the mingling of the "natives" with Britishers, especially Scotsmen, and with Jews: "Although the Jews as a people have never particularly distinguished themselves in literature and science they nevertheless have excellent qualities if only these were properly recognized . . ." William Francis Lynch (1848), the U.S. naval officer celebrated for his account of his voyage of discovery to the River Jordan and Dead Sea, saw the only hope for Palestine in the dissolu-

[34] French poet (1790–1869)
[35] Traveler (1810–1873)
[36] Traveler (1805–1852)
[37] Traveler (1809–1854)

tion of the degenerate Ottoman Empire and the settlement of the Jews.

Active in assisting Jews to settle was James Finn (1853–56), who as British consul in Jerusalem made himself their protector. His own book and his consular reports are prime sources for knowledge of conditions. Among other events he describes the blood libel raised against the Jews.

Henry Baker Tristram (1863–64), English theologian, fellow of the Royal Society, and among the founders of the Palestine Exploration Fund, finds place in his important works on the flora and fauna of Palestine for descriptions of the Jews. But the most interesting of all for that period is the diplomat and statesman Laurence Oliphant (1883–87) who gives a first hand account of the earliest pioneers of the modern resettlement, whom he greatly assisted.

Subsequently there are accounts of historians, theologians, journalists, surveyors, and archaeologists, from all over Europe and the United States, reference to which may be found among the records of the various scientific institutions. Visitors of literary fame who wrote of their impressions include W. M. Thackeray, Mark Twain, George Moore, G. K. Chesterton, Pierre Loti, and Herman Melville.

The flood of books by pilgrims of all kinds and all intentions and pretensions in recent times is overwhelming. As with the earlier pilgrims, the accounts of many of them are colored by their preconceived opinions. Other contemporary writers convey their experiences in the form of novels, detective stories, and thrillers, experiences which are often observed more authentically than in more solemn works.

GLOSSARY

Agudat Israel, world Jewish movement and political party seeking to preserve Orthodoxy by adherence to halakhah as the principle governing Jewish life and society, founded in 1912.

Agunah, woman unable to remarry according to Jewish law, because of desertion by husband or inability to accept presumption of death.

Amora (pl. **amoraim**), title given to the Jewish scholars in Erez Israel and Babylonia in the 3rd and 6th centuries who were responsible for the *Gemara.*

Ashkenazi (pl. **Ashkenazim**), German or West-, Central-, or East-European Jew(s).

Avodah (lit. "service"), sacrificial ritual in the Temple on the Day of Atonement.

Bar mitzvah, ceremony marking the initiation of a boy at the age of 13 into the Jewish religious community.

Bet din (pl. **battei din**), rabbinic court of law.

Capitulations, treaties signed by the Ottoman sultans and the Christian states of Europe concerning the extraterritorial rights which the subjects of one of the signatories would enjoy while staying in the state of another.

Day of Atonement, a day of fasting and atonement, occurring on the tenth of the month of Tishri.

Dayyan (pl. **dayyanim**), member of rabbinic court.

Din, a law (both secular and religious), legal decision, or lawsuit.

Eruv, term applied to various symbolical acts which facilitate the accomplishment of otherwise forbidden acts on the Sabbath and festivals.

Even ha-Ezer, 3rd part of the Shulḥan Arukh dealing with women, marriage, etc.

Firman, a decree or mandate, order, license, or grant issued by the ruler of an oriental country.

Gaon (pl. **geonim**), head of academy in post-Talmudic period, especially in Babylonia; in modern times title given to famous talmudic scholars.

Ḥag (pl. **ḥaggim**), feast.

Haganah, clandestine Jewish organization for armed self-defense in Erez Israel under the British Mandate.

Haggadah, ritual recited in the home on Passover eve at *seder* table.

Ḥakham, title of rabbi of Sephardi congregation.

Ḥakham bashi, title in the 15th cent. and modern times of the chief rabbi in the Ottoman Empire, residing in Constantinople (Istanbul), also applied to principal rabbis in provincial towns.

Halakhah (pl. **halakhot**), an accepted decision in rabbinic law. Also refers to those parts of the Talmud concerned with legal matters.

Ḥaliẓah, in Jewish law ceremony performed when a man refuses to marry his brother's childless widow.

Ḥanafi, an orthodox school of Muslim jurisprudence.

Ḥasid (pl. **ḥasidim**), adherent of Ḥasidism.

Ḥeder (pl. **ḥadarim**), (lit. "room"), school for teaching children Jewish religious observance.

Heikhal Shlomo, a building in Jerusalem that houses the offices of the Chief Rabbinate.

Herem, excommunication, imposed by rabbinical authorities.

Ḥevra kaddisha, associations for burial of the dead.

Ḥoshen Mishpat, 4th part of the Shulḥan Arukh dealing with civil, criminal law, court procedure, etc.

Jewish Agency, international, nongovernment body, centered in Jerusalem, which is the executive and representative of the World Zionist Organization, established in August 1929.

Kasher, ritually permissible food.

Kashrut, Jewish dietary laws.

Kilayim, mixed species: mixed seeds, grafting trees, seeds in vineyard, crossbreeding of animals, the pulling or leading of cattle, wool and linen in the same web. These mixtures are forbidden in Jewish law.

Knesset, parliament of the State of Israel.

Kolel, community in Erez Israel of persons from a particular country or locality, often supported by their fellow countrymen in the Diaspora.

Lag ba-Omer, 33rd (Heb. Lag) day of the Omer period falling on the 18th of Iyyar.

Maḥzor (pl. **maḥzorim**), festival prayer book.

Mejelle, a Turkish code containing rules of law and maxims of Muhammadan jurisprudence.

Mezuzah (pl. **mezuzot**), parchment scroll with selected Torah verses placed in container and affixed to doorposts of rooms occupied by Jews.

Minyan, group of ten male adult Jews, the minimum required for communal prayer.

Mishnah, earliest codification of Jewish Oral Law.

Mitnagged (pl. **Mitnaggedim**), opponents of Ḥasidism.

Mitzvah, biblical or rabbinic injunction.

Mizrachi, religious Zionist movement founded in 1902.

Moshav, smallholders' cooperative agricultural settlement in Israel.

Naḥal, fighting pioneer youth, a regular unit of Israel Defense Forces that educates its members towards cooperative agricultural settlement in Erez Israel.

Neturei Karta (Aramaic "guardians of the city"), group of ultra religious extremists, mainly in Jerusalem, who regard the establishment of a secular Jewish state in Erez Israel as a sin and a denial of God, and therefore do not recognize the State of Israel. Neturei Karta broke away from Agudat Israel in 1935.

Oleh, a Jew coming from the Diaspora to settle in Erez Israel.

Omer, first sheaf cut during barley harvest.

Orlah, the fruit of the trees of the first three years. Their consumption is forbidden in Jewish law.

Posek (pl. **posekim**), codifier or rabbinic scholar who pronounces decisions in disputes and on questions of Jewish law.

Qadi, a Muslim judge.

Rashei Yeshivot, heads of Yeshivot.

Rishon le-Zion, title given to Sephardi chief rabbi in Erez Israel.

Seder, ceremony observed in the Jewish home on the first night of Passover (outside Erez Israel first two nights).

Sephardi (pl. **Sephardim**), Jew(s) of Spain and Portugal and their descendants, wherever resident.

Shafi, an orthodox school of Muslim jurisprudence.

Shariʿa, the body of formally established sacred law in Islam.

Shekhinah, Divine Presence.

Shekhiv mera, dangerously ill person.

196 **Shiur** (pl. **shiurim**), talmudic discourse.

Shofar, horn of the ram (or any other ritually clean animal excepting the cow) sounded for the memorial blowing on Rosh ha-Shanah, and other occasions.

Shohet (pl. **shohatim**), person qualified to perform ritual slaughtering of animals.

Shulhan Arukh, Joseph Caro's code of Jewish law (1564–65) in four parts.

Sublime Porte, cognomen of the Turkish sultan.

Sufi, Muslim mystical movement.

Sunnite, a Muslim belonging to the Sunni branch of Islam—i.e., the body of Islamic custom and practice based on Muhammad's words and deeds.

Sura (Ar.), chapter of the Koran.

Talmud torah, term generally applied to Jewish religious (and ultimately to talmudic) study; also to traditional Jewish religious public schools.

Tanna (pl. **tannaim**), rabbinic teacher of mishnaic period.

Torah, Pentateuch or the Pentateuchal scroll for reading in synagogue.

Waqf, Muslim religious trust.

Yeshivah (pl. **yeshivot**), Jewish traditional academy devoted primarily to study of rabbinic literature.

Yishuv, the Jewish community in Erez Israel in the pre-State period.

Young Turks, a political movement in Turkey founded in 1894.

Zaddik, person outstanding for his faith and piety.

Zedakah, charity.

Zionist Commission, a commission headed by Chaim Weizmann, which proceeded in April 1918 to British-occupied Palestine.

ABBREVIATIONS

Acts	Acts of the Apostles (New Testament)
A.H.	After *Hijra* (*Hijra* = Islamic era beginning in 622 C.E.)
ARN[1]	Avot de-Rabbi Nathan, version(1)
Bik.	*Bikkurim* (talmudic tractate)
Chron.	Chronicles (Bible)
Deut.	Deuteronomy (Bible)
Ep.	Epistle
Ex.	Exodus (Bible)
Ex. R.	Exodus Rabbah
Gal.	Epistle to the Galatians (New Testament)
Ḥag.	*Ḥagigah* (talmudic tractate)
Isa.	Isaiah (Bible)
Jos. Ant.	Josephus, *Jewish Antiquities*
Jos. Wars	Josephus, *The Jewish Wars*
Lam. R.	Lamentations Rabbah
Ma'as. Sh.	*Ma' aser Sheni* (talmudic tractate)
Meg.	*Megillah* (talmudic tractate)
MK	*Mo'ed Katan* (talmudic tractate)
Ned.	*Nedarim* (talmudic tractate)
Num. R.	Numbers Rabbah
Pes.	*Pesaḥim* (talmudic tractate)
Ps.	Psalms (Bible)
Rev.	Revelation (New Testament)
Shevu.	*Shevu'ot* (talmudic tractate)
Spec.	Philo, *De Specialibus Legibus*
Suk.	*Sukkah* (talmudic tractate)
TJ	Jerusalem Talmud
Tosef.	Tosefta
Zep.	Zephaniah (Bible)
Zev.	*Zevaḥim* (talmudic tractate)

BIBLIOGRAPHICAL ABBREVIATIONS

AJSLL	*American Journal of Semitic Languages and Literature* (1884–)
Alon, Meḥkarim	G. Alon, *Meḥkarim be-Toledot Yisrael bi-Ymei Bayit Sheni u-vi-Tekufat ha-Mishnah ve-ha-Talmud*, 2 vols. (1957–58)
Alon, Toledot²	G. Alon, *Toledot ha-Yehudim be-Erez Yisrael bi-Tekufat ha-Mishnah ve-ha-Talmud*, 1 (1958³), 2 (1961²)
BA	*Biblical Archaeologist* (1938ff.)
Baron, Community	S. W. Baron, *The Jewish Community, its History and Structure to the American Revolution*, 3 vols. (1942)
Baron, Social	S. W. Baron, *Social and Religious History of the Jews*, 3 vols. (1937); enlarged, 1–2 (1952²), 3–14 (1957–69)
Ben-Zvi, Erez	I. Ben-Zvi, *Erez Yisrael bi-Ymei ha-Shilton ha-Otomani*, (1955)
BZAW	*Beihefte zur Zeitschrift fuer die alttestamentliche Wissenschaft*, supplement to ZAW (1896ff.)
EI²	*Encyclopaedia of Islam*, second edition (1954–68)
Finkelstein, Middle Ages	L. Finkelstein, *Jewish Self-Government in the Middle Ages* (1924)
Gulak, Yesodei	A. Gulak, *Yesodei ha-Mishpat ha-Ivri*, 4 vols. (1922; repr. 1967)
HTR	*Harvard Theological Review* (1908ff.)
HUCA	*Hebrew Union College Annual* (1904; 1924ff.)
ILR	*Israel Law Review* (1966ff.)

JA	*Journal asiatique* (1822ff.)
JQR	*Jewish Quarterly Review* (1889ff.)
KS	*Kirjath Sepher* (1923/24ff.)
Mann, Texts	J. Mann, *Texts and Studies,* 2 vols. (1931–35)
PAAJR	*Proceedings of the American Academy for Jewish Research* (1930ff.)
REJ	*Revue des études juives* (1880ff.)
Ya'ari, Sheluḥei	A. Ya'ari, *Sheluḥei Ereẓ Yisrael* (1951)

BIBLIOGRAPHY

Jews: Abraham M. Luncz, *Lu'aḥ Yerushalayim,* 13 vols. (1896–1916); idem, *Yerushalayim,* 20 vols. (1882–1916); D.N. Brinker, *Lu'ah Yerushalayim,* 11 vols. (1941–1952); Israel, Government Year Book (1950–   ), Ministry of Religious Affairs, Reports; Ha-Maḥlakah le-Ḥinnukh ve-Tarbut ba-Golah, *Dat Yisrael u-Medinat Yisrael* (1951); N. Kraus (ed.), *The Encyclopedical Religious Yearbook* (Heb. and Eng., 1962); N. Bentwich, in: A. J. Arberry (ed.), *Religion in the Middle East . . .,* 1 (1969), 59–118; J. Badi, *Religion in Israel Today . . .* (1959); H. Weiner, *Wild Goats of En-Gedi* (1963⁶); E. Goldman, *Religious Issues in Israel's Political Life* (1964); Mizrachi World Center, *Religion and State in Israel* (1965); M. Ostrovsky, *Irgun ha-Yishuv be-Ereẓ Yisrael* (1942); Y. Even-Ḥen, *Ha-Rabbanut ha-Rashit le-Yisrael be-Avar u-va-Hoveh* (1964); Z. Warhaftig, *Ba'ayot ha-Dat be-Yisrael* (1966). SABBATH AND JEWISH HOLIDAYS: *Sefer ha-Mo'adim, Parashat Mo'adei Yisrael, Erkam, Gilluyeihem ve-Hashpa'atam . . .,* 8 vols. (1956–67). NON-ORTHODOX CONGREGATIONS: S. Ben-Chorin, in: *Journal of Central Conference of American Rabbis* (June, 1962), 3–11; J. Kaufman, *ibid.* (Jan. 1963), 3–9.

Muslims: A. Cohen, *Israel and the Arab World* (1969); A. L. Tibawi, *Arab Education in Mandatory Palestine* (1956), index; Y. Waschitz and M. Zubi, in: *Ha-Mizraḥ he-Ḥadash,* 15 (1965), 85–92; A. Yinnon, *ibid.,* 57–84; 16 (1966), 349–80; *Israel Government Year Books.*

Christians: C. Copp, *Holy Places of the Gospels* (1963); C. Wardi (ed.), *Christians in Israel. A Survey* (1950); L. G. A. Gust, *Status Quo in the Holy Places* (1930); S. Colbi, *Christianity in the*

Holy Land (1969); B. Bagatti, *L'Eglise de la Gentilité en Palestine* (1968); idem, *L'Eglise de la Circoncision* (1965); B. Collin, *Les Lieux Saints* (1948); N. Moschopoulos, *La Terre Sainte* (1957); Israel Ministry of Religious Affairs, *Christian News from Israel* (1949–).

Samaritans: C. D. Mantel, in: *Bar Ilan, Sefer ha-Shanah,* 7–8 (1970), 162–77; Montgomery, *The Samaritans* (1907, 1968); I. Ben-Zvi, *Sefer ha-Shomronim* (1970²); R. Tsedaka, *Samaritan Legends (Aggadot Am Shomroniyyot)* (1965), 33–56, 86–88; Ben-Zvi, *Erez Yisrael,* 419–30; R. Kirchheim, *Karmei Shomron* (1851, 1970), 1–54; M. Ish-Shalom, *Masei ha-Nozerim le-Erez Yisrael* (1966), index s.v. *Shomronim;* I. Ben-Hanania, in: *Yedi'ot ha-Ḥevrah la-Ḥakirot Erez Yisrael va-Attikoteha,* 11 no. 3–4 (1945), 57–63; B. Tsedaka, in: *Ba-Ma'arakhah* (1969); J. Macdonald, *The Theology of the Samaritans* (1964); M. Haran, in: *Eretz Israel,* 4 (1956), 160–9; A. S. Halkin, in: *Goldziher Memorial Volume* (1958), 86–100. NEW YEAR AND DAY OF ATONEMENT: B. Tsedaka, in: *Ba-Ma'arakhah,* 101 (1969); R. Tsedaka, *Siddurei Tefillot Mo'ed ha-Ḥodesh ha-Shevi'i, Shabbat Aseret Yemei ha-Seliḥot u-Mo'ed Yom ha-Kippur* (1963) (in Samaritan-Hebrew letters). THE FEAST OF TABERNACLES AND SHEMINI AZERET: B. Tsedaka, in: *Ba-Ma'arakhah,* 97 (1969); 102 (1969); I. Tsedaka, *Siddur Tefillat Ḥag ha-Sukkot ve-Shabbat Mo'ed Ḥag ha-Sukkot* (1963); D. J. Boys, in: *London Quarterly and Wolborn Review* (1961); 32–37; R. Tsedaka, *The Prayer of the Ten Commandments* (in Samaritan Hebrew letters; 1962). PASSOVER: *Pesach on Hargrizim. The Samaritans;* special edition of the Samaritan newspaper *"A-B—The Samaritan News"* (n. d.). SHAVUOT: B. Tsedaka, in: *Ba-Ma'arakhah,* 98 (1969).

Karaites: R. Mahler, *Kara'im* (Yid., 1947, Heb., 1949); L. Nemoy, *Karaite Anthology* (1952); Z. Ankori, *Karaites in Byzantium* (1959), includes extensive bibliography, 461–84; idem, in: *Essays on Jewish Life and Thought . . . in Honor of S. W. Baron* (1959), 1–38; idem, in: *Tarbiz,* 29(1959/60), 195–202;30(1960/61), 186–208; Grajewsky, *Me-Ḥayyei ha-Kara'im bi-Yrushalayim* (1922); S. Assaf, in: *Tarbiz,* 4 (1932/33), 35–53, 193–206; idem, *Be-Oholei Ya'akov* (1943), 181–222; Z. Cohn, *The Halakah of the Karaites* (1936); idem, *The Rise of the Karaite Sect* (1937);

I. Ben Zvi, in: KS, 32 (1956/57), 366–74; idem, *Meḥkarim u-Mekorot* (1966), 267–78; P. S. Goldberg, *Karaite Liturgy and its Relation to Synagogue* (1957); Dinur, Golah, 4 (1962), index, 601; J. Rosenthal, in: *Sefer ha-Yovel . . . H. Albeck* (1963), 425–42 (= *Meḥkarim u-Mekorot*, 1 (1967), 234–52); idem, in: KS, 36 (1963/64), 59–63; C. Roth, in: *Yerushalayim*, 4 (1953), 138–40.

The Druze: Sprengling, in: AJSLL, 56 (1939), 388–414; EI², 2 (1962²), 136–7, 631–4; H. Blanc, *Ha-Deruzim* (1958); M. von Oppenheim, *Vom Mittelmeer zum Persischen Golf*, 1 (1899), 110ff.; E. N. Adler, *Itinerary of Benjamin of Tudela* (1907), 20 (Heb. sect.), 18 (Eng. sect.); H.Z. Hirschberg, *Religion in the Middle East*, 2 (1968), 330–48.

The Bahā'ī: J. Ferraby, *All Things Made New; A Comprehensive Outline of the Bahai Faith* (1957); *The Bahai Faith 1844–1963, Information Statistical and Comparative* (pamphlet), with addendum to 1964; *The Bahā'ī World*, vol. 13 (1954–63), 1970, edited by the Universal House of Justice, an authoritative source for the history of the Faith.

Legal and Judicial System: Gulak, Yesodei, 1(1922), 3–31; 4 (1922), 3–45; S. Assaf, *Ha-Onshin Aḥarei Hatimat ha-Talmud* (1922); idem, *Battei ha-Din ve-Sidreihem . . .* (1924); A. H. Freimann, in: *Lu'aḥ ha-Arez* (1945/46), 110–25; H. Cohen, in: *Ha-Peraklit*, 3 (1946), 38 ff.; Baron, Community; Hebrew Law and the State of Israel: a Symposium, in: *Sura*, 3 (1975/58), 457–518; Alon, Toledot²; Alon, Meḥkarim; M. Silberg, *Kakh Darko shel Talmud* (1961), 66ff.; Finkelstein, Middle Ages; M. Elon, *Ḥerut ha-Perat be-Darkhei Geviyyat Ḥov . . .* (1964), 11–14 (introd.), 255–69; idem, in: ILR, 2 (1967), 515–65; 3 (1968), 88–126; 416–57; 4 (1969), 80–140; idem, in: *Ha-Peraklit*, 25 (1968/69), 27–53; idem, *Ḥakikah Datit . . .* (1968); B. Cohen, *Jewish and Roman Law*, 2 vols. (1966); J. I. Englard, in: ILR, 3 (1968), 254–78.

Holy Places: M. Ish-Shalom, *Kivrei Avot* (1948); Z. Vilnay, *Maẓẓevot Kodesh be-Erez Yisrael* (1951), incl. bibl. for Jewish graves; J. Parkes, *History of Palestine* (1949), 370ff., incl. bibl.; T. Canaan, *Mohammedan Saints and Sanctuaries in Palestine* (1927); S. P. Colbi, *Christianity in the Holy Land, Past and Present* (1969); H. Lauterpacht, *Jerusalem and the Holy Places* (1968); B. Collin, *Le problème juridique des Lieux-Saints* (1956). 203

Western Wall: A. M. Luncz, in: *Yerushalayim,* 10 (1913), 1–58; idem, in: *Lu'ah Erez Yisrael,* 20/21 (1914–15–16), 1–8; *The Western or Wailing Wall in Jerusalem;* Memorandum by the Secretary of State for the Colonies, Cmd. 3229 (1928); *Protocol of the 14th Session of the Permanent Mandates Commission of the League of Nations* (1928), 205–7; C. Adler, *Memorandum on the Western Wall* (1930); *Report of the Commission of the Palestine Disturbances of August 1929,* Cmd. 3530 (1930); J. Ya'ari-Poleskin, *Baron Edmond Rothschild,* 1 (Heb., 1930), 206–19; J. Triwaks, *Mishpat ha-Kotel* (1931); C. D. Matthews, in: *The Muslim World,* 22 (1932), 331–9; P. Grayewsky, *Sippurei Kotel ha-Ma'aravi* (1936); E. R. Malachi, in: *Lu'ah Yerushalayim* 12 (1951/52), 275–81; Z. Vilnay, *Yerushalayim—Ha-Ir ha-Attikah* (1967³), 97–109; M. Hacohen, *Ha-Kotel ha-Ma'aravi* (1968²); M. Natan, *Ha-Milhamah al Yerushalayim* (1968⁶), 311–21; M. Har El, *Zot Yerushalayim* (1969), 229–40; M. A. Druck and Z. Steiner (eds.), *Album ha-Kotel ha-Ma'aravi* (1969).

Pilgrimage: SECOND TEMPLE PERIOD: I. Elbogen, in: *der Hochschule fuer die Wissenschaft des Judentums,* 46 (1929), 27–46; S. Safrai, in: *Sefer Yerushalayim,* ed. by M. Avi-Yonah, 1 (1956), 369–91; idem, in: *Zion,* 25 (1959/60), 67–84. POST-TEMPLE PERIOD: K. Wilhelm, *Roads to Zion* (1948); S. Assaf and A. L. Mayer, *Sefer ha-Yishuv,* 2 (1944), 25–29; A. Yaari, in : KS, 18 (1941/42), 293–7, 378–80; idem, *Iggerot Erez Yisrael* (1943); idem, *Masot Erez Yisrael* (1946); Ya'ari, Sheluhei, index; M. A. Shulvass, *Roma vi-Yrushalayim* (1944), passim; idem, in: *Zion,* 3 (1938), 86–7; S. A. Horodezky, *Olei Ziyyon* (1947); S. Assaf, *Tekufat ha-Ge'onim ve-Sifrutah* (1955), 91–7; R. Mahler, *Divrei Yemei Yisrael* (1956), 117–31; Ben-Zvi, Erez Yisrael (1967³); S. Safrai, *Ha-Aliyyah le-Regel bi-Ymei ha-Bayit ha-Sheni* (1966); Ta-Shema, in: *Tarbiz,* 38 (1968/69), 398–9. CHRISTIAN PILGRIMAGES: R. Roericht, *Bibliotheca Geographica Palaestina* (new ed., 1963); P. Thomsen, *Palaestina-Literatur* (1908, 1956, 1960); T. Wright (ed.), *Early Travels in Palestine* (1948); M. Ish-Shalom, *Masei ha-Nozerim le-Erez Yisrael* (1966); T. Kollek and M. Pearlman, *Pilgrims to the Holy Land* (1970).

INDEX

206

210